SEAMUS HEANEY

Seamus Heaney [signature]

A LIFE WELL WRITTEN

❦

RAND BRANDES

❦

SELECTIONS *from the* COLLECTIONS

of CAROLYN *&* WARD SMITH,

ALAN M. KLEIN, *and* RAND BRANDES

❦

EXHIBITED *at*

THE GROLIER CLUB

SEPTEMBER 10 — NOVEMBER 1

❦

THE GROLIER CLUB

New York

LENOIR-RHYNE UNIVERSITY

Hickory, North Carolina

❦

2014

ISBN 978-0-9905607-0-8

FRONTISPIECE:
Seamus Heaney, late 1980s,
Toner's Bog, Northern Ireland,
photographed by Rand Brandes.
It had just begun to rain.

CONTENTS

Illustration for "Door into the Dark" from Poems and a Memoir, *1982.*

꘎

WE FIRST BECAME AWARE of Seamus Heaney's work when Ward was given a book of his poems. We have separate collecting interests, but both of us thought this was a poet whose work we would enjoy collecting together. This exhibition was originally planned to celebrate the poet's seventy-fifth birthday year. However, we have reconfigured it to celebrate his extraordinary life. We are delighted to be working with fellow Grolier Club member Rand Brandes to curate this exhibition. We would also like to thank Nathan Moehlmann for his splendid design and production of the catalogue for this show. And we extend a warm thank you to fellow member Alan Klein for lending material to the exhibition.

When we began, in the early 1980s, there was no bibliography and not much other information about the publication of his work. We avidly attended any poetry reading he gave — at our first one there were only about a dozen of us in attendance. Over the years, Heaney's readings were standing room only events. We began scouting bookstores wherever we traveled as well as in New York City. Surprisingly, there was little to be found in Dublin. However, the few items we did find were early items casually tucked away on random shelves.

Often, the idea of buying his work (prior to his Nobel Prize) was treated dismissively by many dealers. After The Prize was awarded, many dealers complained at the paucity of material available and that it would go out the shop as rapidly as it came in. On one London trip, we were exploring a shop that had nothing available that we didn't already have. As we were about to leave, the dealer said he had a few items from his personal collection that he hadn't planned to sell. However, business had been slow and so he sold us some Christmas cards that Heaney had sent to his editor, Charles Monteith, of Faber and Faber. News travels fast in the booksellers' community. When we returned to New York City, a dealer was on the phone saying he also had some Christmas cards that we might be interested in.

When we joined the Grolier Club, a knowledgeable resource materialized. This resource was a long-time collector of Heaney's work—James O'Halloran. Jim grew up in Ireland and was a friend of many Irish poets. He was generous with his information and with the names of dealers and institutions who might have Heaney material. We discovered other Seamus Heaney fans in the Club and they also added to our information base. In 2008, the publication of the Heaney bibliography, written by Rand Brandes and Michael J. Durkan, gave us detailed information about his work from 1959 to 2003. For the period of time since 2003, we have again had to rely on our own resources and the work of a few book dealers and friends to find the material we wished to add to our collection. Over the years, in the hope that there was the possibility of a broadside or booklet to commemorate his visit, we have also called colleges and other institutions when we heard that Heaney might be present or coming.

We began with just the books, but were soon captivated by the broadsides, Christmas cards, and other ephemera. Over time, we also added many periodicals, a number of which published poems before they were included in the books. We discovered *Gorgon*, where, in 1959, an untested Heaney published a poem under the pseudonym Incertus. We also found some very early broadsheets, where he and other poets printed some of their early work. As a budding poet, he participated in a poetry discussion group in Northern Ireland led initially by Philip Hobsbaum and then by Heaney. Mimeographed sheets of poetry, one set of which is on display, were shared with other poets for comments and critique.

Seamus Heaney was generous with his poetry. He composed many poems for special occasions such as birthdays, awards, anniversaries, and the like. Many of these have been published in small editions and generally in wrappers. Some have been printed on broadsides.

He also worked with many artists, and together they produced beautiful *livres d'artistes* and broadsides. He enjoyed translating poetic works into English and often these translations were published with original art work.

The appeal of Heaney's work lies in his command of and innovative use of the English language. Rooted in his childhood in Ireland and enhanced by his encounters with other poets and time teaching abroad, he developed a distinctive voice, which evokes his roots and his life. He had begun to memorize poetry at an early age and read it avidly throughout his life. He understood well the power of verse.

His iconic poem, "Digging," compares his work with that of his father digging in his garden:

Between my finger and my thumb
The squat pen rests; snug as a gun.

Under my window, a clean rasping sound
When the spade sinks into gravelly ground;
My father, digging. [. . .]

By God, the old man could handle a spade.
Just like his old man. [. . .]

But I've no spade to follow men like them.

Between my finger and my thumb
The squat pen rests.
I'll dig with it.

He dug extremely well.

— WARD *&* CAROLYN SMITH

Title page from The Light of the Leaves, *1999.*

W HEN CAROLYN AND WARD SMITH and I first talked of a "members exhibition" of our Heaney collections, our title was *Seamus Heaney: A Life Well Lived*. It was to be an exhibition marking the Nobel Laureate's seventy-fifth birthday in 2014. That all changed with the unexpected passing of Seamus Heaney last year on August 30, 2013. I attended Seamus Heaney's funeral in Dublin where I had been graciously welcomed by the Heaney family. After much soul-searching, the Smiths and I decided to proceed with the exhibition and approach it as an appreciation of the poet's life in print and as a testament to the ongoing power of his poetry. Thus, the exhibition title: *Seamus Heaney: A Life Well Written*.

The last time I saw Seamus was in March 2013 at the opening of Emory University's outstanding Heaney exhibition, *The Music of What Happens*, curated by Geraldine Higgins. The poet was in great form with several writing projects in the works and a full traveling schedule ahead of him. As Seamus graciously made his way among the displays, I was looking forward to a similar experience at the Grolier Club. I know that he would be pleased with the exhibition we have assembled out of our collections, appreciating its attention to detail and design as well as the personal relationships that weave their way from case to case.

SEAMUS HEANEY LOVED BOOKS, well-written and profound books, the books that formed the canon and those that challenged and changed the canon. He also loved the books (and comic books) of his childhood, often using their covers and illustrations as touch-stones for deeper memories and meditations. The books could be used, beaten and battered, but it was their physicality that mattered. In one of his later poems, "Route 11" from *Human Chain*, it is the narrator's wandering through a used bookstore in Belfast where he purchases a copy of *The Aeneid*, that sets him off on a Virgilian jour-ney to the underworld. Heaney also had a great appreciation for the spiritual discipline and artistic talents of ancient Irish scribes and illuminators and used their lives, talents, materials, and tools as metaphors for his own life as a writer.

By the time Heaney published his first books in the 1960s, he was already benefitting from the renewed interest in Europe and America in small presses, artisan materials, and limited editions. In fact, he had sent a manuscript of what would become in a different form his first book, *Death of a Naturalist*, to Liam Miller of the Dolmen Press. This Irish press drew its lineage directly from Cuala Press, which was operated by W. B. Yeats and his sisters during the Irish Literary Revival. Though *Death of a Naturalist* was published in London by Faber, Heaney was very loyal to his cultural heritage and consciously published regularly with Gallery Press, the most important publisher of poetry in Ireland, and he helped to establish the Field Day Theatre Company, which developed its own imprint in Derry, Northern Ireland, in the late 1980s.

One reason that Seamus Heaney's reputation grew so rapidly in the U.S. was because he became caught up in the "Greening of America" that began in the 1960s and 1970s. Suddenly all things Irish became counter-cultural and cool, even the violence in Northern Ireland when seen as part of a growing global demand for civil rights and self-determination. Professional organizations like the American Conference for Irish Studies offered a more sophisticated and subversive understanding of "Irishness" drawing heavily upon "new" readings of Irish writers like Joyce and Yeats. It soon appeared that an industry driven by scholars, booksellers, museums and summer schools had been built out of and around these writers and their works. Seamus Heaney was aware of his precarious position in relation to this industrial impulse and the commodification of Irish culture. He was also alert to a similar multinational enterprise in the world of fine books and prints that was beginning to advance on his own work.

As in many aspects of his life as represented in his poetry, Heaney had to navigate between his deep appreciation for the interest shown in his work from students, scholars, publishers, artists, and collectors with his need for privacy and a true humility that grounded his life and writing. Like all great artists, he fiercely protected the mystery of his art and its vital sources. His relationship with publishers and collectors was particularly complicated. Generous to a fault and always respectful, many of the limited editions of his work, especially in his later years, originated in projects designed to benefit specific non-profit organizations or to recognize or memorialize a long-term friendship, admiration, or association. Other limited editions, however, came from the pleasure he derived from seeing his poems in new settings, new bindings, and in the company of inspiring images. At the end of the day, Heaney shared the same aesthetic impulses and satisfactions that his publishers and collectors of his work experienced. This appreciation was always within the context of wanting to be sure that these publications served the poems and not the other way around.

For the Nobel prize-winning poet, books, the physical, material objects, were an endless source of pleasure — a pleasure not too far removed from the original pleasure of poetic creation. Like all writers, Heaney experienced a sustaining satisfaction when the thoughts and feelings and experiences that formed mysteriously deep inside him found expression in print and on the page.

AS NOTED, COLLECTING THE WORKS of living authors is complicated, as is making them the object of one's scholarly research. There is always the issue of proximity and where the collector's or scholar's connection falls on the poet's professional–personal gamut. Seamus Heaney was always so gracious and generous when asked for an autograph or the donation of a poem to a worthy publishing project that one immediately felt "close" to him. Correspondingly, he was loyal to his publishers and his professional hosts, and until late in his life Heaney would sometimes sign books for hours. Unfortunately, some people in the book business would joke about a Heaney publication that was "rare in the unsigned state" — a condition that has certain market implications for them. Seamus Heaney never followed the "Heaney market," but he knew that it existed and accepted the commodification of his work as an inevitable reality of the publishing business.

Regardless of the imperatives of the marketplace, Heaney's friendliness and approachability are legendary. You can count on one hand the number of known first-class privately held Heaney collections, and the poet was aware of those involved in assembling them. He showed a particular affection for the Smiths as well as for fellow Grolier members and Heaney collectors Jim O'Halloran and Ron Schuchard. The Smiths have one of the strongest and most complete private collections in the world of Heaney books, pamphlets, broadsides, and cards. It has been a joy to spend time with them (both the Smiths and the publications) over the past few years. Seamus was pleased to know of the Smiths' collection because he considered them good people and knew that his works were in good hands.

My Heaney collection, on the other hand, has a clearly academic orientation in that I concentrated on first appearances of poems and essays in periodicals and contributions to books. I have used these publications in several academic articles to discuss Heaney's editing process as well as his publishing practices. I have also relied heavily on these publications for my work-in-progress: *A Commentary on the Collected Poems of Seamus Heaney*. My collection also includes many rare (or not) publications with substantial or significant inscriptions by Seamus Heaney to me and members of my family. One item that I could not part with for the exhibition, but of which I am particularly honored to have, is the poem "The Rainstick" in a large format and in the poet's hand. Heaney dedicated the poem to "Beth and Rand," and it first appeared in the *New Republic* in 1993. It is the first poem in Heaney's volume *The Spirit Level* (1996).

I have known the Heaney family for over thirty years and worked on several projects with Seamus's full cooperation and encouragement, including *Seamus Heaney: A Reference Guide* (G. K. Hall, 1996) and *Seamus Heaney: A Bibliography 1959–2003* (Faber, 2008). Both publications were co-edited by the late Michael J. Durkan. At the time of his death in 1996, Michael had been compiling a bibliography of Heaney's primary works, and I had been using similar bibliographical materials for a commentary on the collected poems of Seamus Heaney. I had already spent the 1993–1994 academic year with my family in Dublin as a Fulbright Fellow helping Seamus organize, document, and preserve his manuscripts, which were in the attic of his home on Sandymount Strand. Seamus asked me if I would be willing to take over the bibliography project following the death of Michael Durkan. Heaney knew that I was not a certified bibliographer, but he trusted me and had faith in my ability to learn along the way. He also committed himself to the project, notifying me of new publications and occasionally sending on copies.

The descriptions of the Seamus Heaney items that follow in *Seamus Heaney: A Life Well Written* are impressionistic. I did not want to reproduce the technical bibliographical descriptions that appear in *Seamus Heaney: A Bibliography 1959–2003*, many of which benefitted from Jim O'Halloran's expertise and were based upon Heaney items in O'Halloran's now disassembled collection. Instead, I wanted to provide a living context that would animate the items. This contextual concoction is a mixture of personal, publishing, cultural, and historical information, with a touch of speculation when appropriate. The exhibition items cover the entirety of Heaney's publishing life from 1959 to 2013. We have also selected works that demonstrate the range of Heaney's publications, from trade editions with multiple covers to limited editions to extremely rare editions in a rich variety of bindings and formats. The unpublished items in the exhibition provide a glimpse into Heaney's life as a poet. We hope that when taken in its totality, the exhibition gives one the sense of how "well-written" Seamus Heaney's life was and how enduring his contributions to the world of poetry will continue to be.

※

WE THANK LENOIR-RHYNE UNIVERSITY, in Hickory, North Carolina, for their support of *Seamus Heaney: A Life Well Written*; Nathan Moehlmann of Goosepen Studio *&* Press for his exceptional work on the exhibition catalogue; and Alan M. Klein, for sharing his copy of *Apparitions*, an early version of Heaney's *Keeping Going*. All of the other Heaney items listed are from the collection of Carolyn and Ward Smith except where otherwise noted as "Brandes."

The majority of information in the item descriptions is drawn directly from *Seamus Heaney: A Bibliography 1959–2003*. In addition to information that appears in a publication's colophon or various prospectuses and introductory materials, I also dipped into *Stepping Stones: Interviews with Seamus Heaney* by Dennis O'Driscoll and *Artists / Heaney / Books: An Exhibition* published by the Irish Museum of Modern Art (2009), which includes an interview with Seamus Heaney by Christina Kennedy. Finally, as a result of Seamus Heaney's global cultural profile, additional information is now considered "general knowledge" and treated as such.

NOSTALGIA IN THE AFTERNOON . .

Great blue-scooped sky, arching above me,   (white
Breeze - winnowed , shell- sounding and bubbling
  With the smooth soap-slip caressing of pot-
                              bellied clouds,
I leap towards your high intangible blueness
            With Gothic agility.

Up above now, widely wheeling in free cool curvings,
The sky is talking to me, and soft whorls of feathery
      cloud- cream lick over my skin: (earth,
Now I smell days spent close to the warm breathing
Here in a firm rounded moment, suspended in
                              swaying space,

        And I live times distilled from time past.

Times when the cuckoo curled lobes of smooth music
        Over sunny acres of hay   (coloured sound
And larks were spilling light pebbles of all
        Sand falling, tumbling. tinkling,
Sound torn ragged and open with a corn-crake's
        Jagged-edge noise,
Rasping backwards and forwards
        As metal through gravel.

Upsurging into the blue scoope of the sky
This rich translucent music, coming through
The lovely objective slant of hot sunlight, (down,
Until the grey billows of night unfurl and roll
Leaving me low on black hard rocks.
                              Incertus

PEACE

The hill like a curled up dog
Heats itself at the fire in the sky;
Sleeping with a thousand summers
In his stomach,
No wish greater than to rest.

Up pile the leaves
That dying do not wish

Page 17 from *Gorgon* (Seamus Heaney's second place of publication, 1959)
where "Nostalgia in the Afternoon" appears (his third published poem) under
his pen name, "Incertus." As a sign of his growing confidence as a poet,
he would not use "Incertus" after 1961.

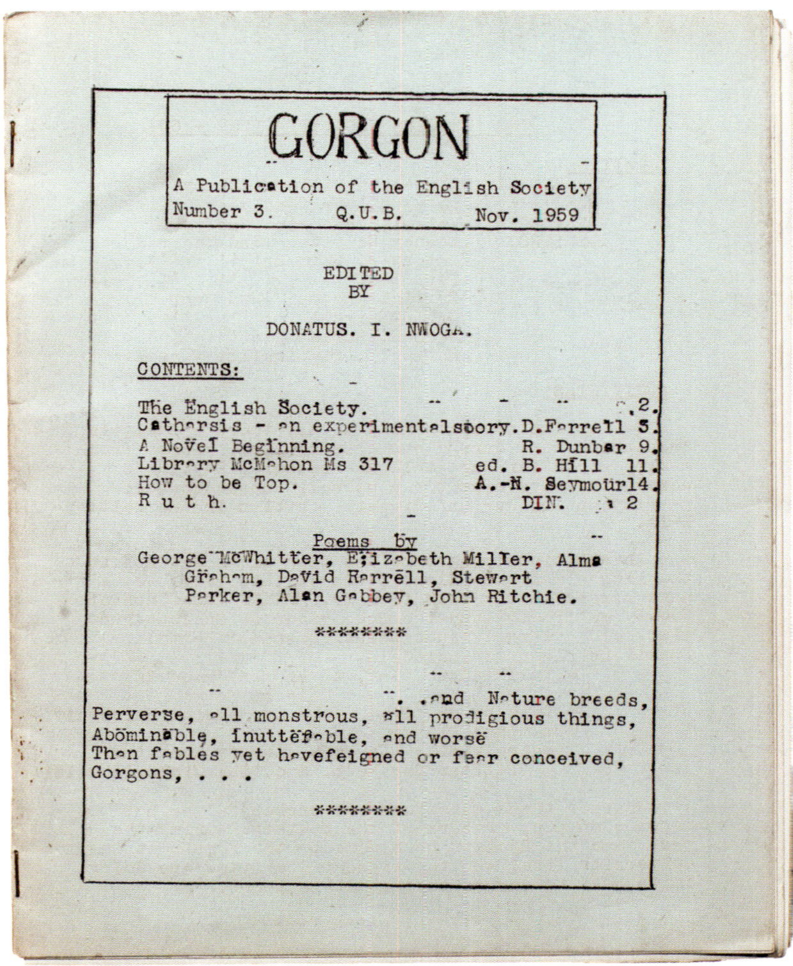

Cover of *Gorgon: A Publication of the English Society*. November 1959, No. 3, Queen's University Belfast, poem "Nostalgia in the Afternoon." by Seamus Heaney under the pen name Incertus, 16.75 × 21 cm.

1 : *Gorgon*

Not surprisingly, Seamus Heaney was an excellent and engaged student throughout the years of his formal education. After leaving Anahorish Primary School in 1951, he won a scholarship to St. Columb's College, which was about sixty miles away in Derry City. The iconic poem, "Midterm Break," describes Heaney being told by the staff at St. Columb's of the death, in 1953, of his younger brother, Christopher, who had been struck by a car near his home. Heaney then attended Queen's University Belfast in 1957 where he became active in the university's literary scene. He published his first poems, "Reaping in the Heat," "October Thought," and "Nostalgia in the Afternoon" in the autumn of 1959 in the university's student publications, *Q* and *Gorgon*. These 1959 poems by Heaney were attributed to "Incertus," as the young poet explored his commitment to the creative life and his confidence in his writing. "Incertus" was not listed on the title page table of contents of *Gorgon*, but the editor's name was, Donatus I. Nwoga, the dedicatee of Heaney's 1992 poem "A Dog Was Crying Tonight in Wicklow Also." Donatus Nwoga, who died in 1991, was a professor of African literature and the dean of the faculty of arts at the University of Nigeria, Nsukka. However, Heaney signed other *Gorgon* poems variously as "Seamus Heaney" or "Seamus J. Heaney." One anomaly of attribution occurs in the 1964 *Irish Times* publication of the poem "Fisher," which lists the author as "James Heaney." ("James" is the English iteration of the Irish "Seamus.") The last poem Heaney published in *Gorgon* was "Her Home" in 1961 — the poem is still attributed to "Incertus." By that time his works were beginning to appear in regional and national literary publications as noted above.

2 : *The Newman*

SEAMUS HEANEY GRADUATED with first-class honors from Queen's University Belfast in 1961. During the 1961–1962 academic year he completed a diploma course at St. Joseph's College of Education, Andersontown, Belfast. As part of his Teacher Training program he taught at St. Thomas's Secondary Intermediate School in Ballymurphy, Belfast. While at St. Thomas he was befriended by the famous Irish short-story writer Michael McLaverty who was the headmaster of the school. While at St. Joseph's, Seamus Heaney was trying his hand at writing essays. His first essay, "Shall We Jive this Jig?" was published in *The Irish Digest* (Dublin) in April 1961. The essay discussed the similarities and differences between the new modern dance style, the jive and traditional Irish dancing, the *ceilidhe*. Later that year he published a curious understated essay on the new chapel at St. Joseph's: "Modern, Functional, Beautiful." The essay appeared in *Newman*, a publication of the Cardinal Newman Society of Queen's University Belfast. In this same issue of *Newman*, Seamus Heaney is listed in the "Who's Who" section of the periodical. It was an auspicious introduction to the world at large for a young poet who would go on to be awarded the Nobel Prize thirty-four years later.

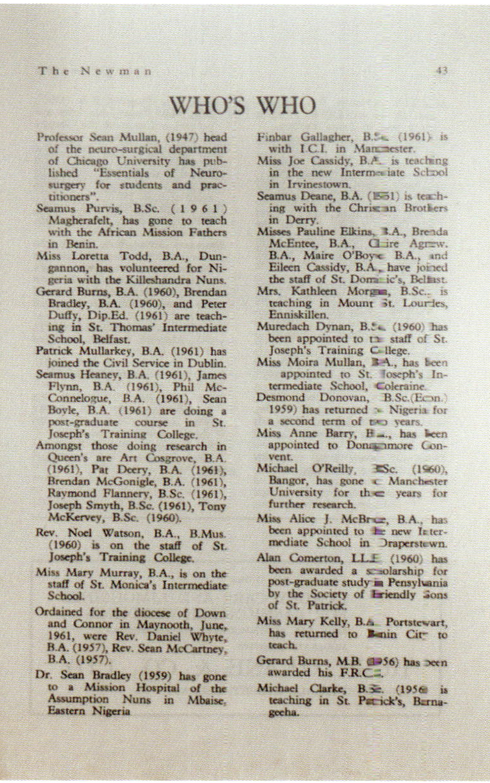

WHO'S WHO

Professor Sean Mullan, (1947) head of the neuro-surgical department of Chicago University has published "Essentials of Neuro-surgery for students and practitioners".

Seamus Purvis, B.Sc. (1961) Magherafelt, has gone to teach with the African Mission Fathers in Benin.

Miss Loretta Todd, B.A., Dungannon, has volunteered for Nigeria with the Killeshandra Nuns.

Gerard Burns, B.A. (1960), Brendan Bradley, B.A. (1960), and Peter Duffy, Dip.Ed. (1961) are teaching in St. Thomas' Intermediate School, Belfast.

Patrick Mullarkey, B.A. (1961) has joined the Civil Service in Dublin.

Seamus Heaney, B.A. (1961), James Flynn, B.A. (1961), Phil McConnelogue, B.A. (1961), Sean Boyle, B.A. (1961) are doing a post-graduate course in St. Joseph's Training College.

Amongst those doing research in Queen's are Art Cosgrove, B.A. (1961), Pat Deery, B.A. (1961), Brendan McGonigle, B.A. (1961), Raymond Flannery, B.Sc. (1961), Joseph Smyth, B.Sc. (1961), Tony McKervey, B.Sc. (1960).

Rev. Noel Watson, B.A., B.Mus. (1960) is on the staff of St. Joseph's Training College.

Miss Mary Murray, B.A., is on the staff of St. Monica's Intermediate School.

Ordained for the diocese of Down and Connor in Maynooth, June, 1961, were Rev. Daniel Whyte, B.A. (1957), Rev. Sean McCartney, B.A. (1957).

Dr. Sean Bradley (1959) has gone to a Mission Hospital of the Assumption Nuns in Mbaise, Eastern Nigeria

Finbar Gallagher, B.Sc. (1961) is with I.C.I. in Manchester.

Miss Joe Cassidy, B.A. is teaching in the new Intermediate School in Irvinestown.

Seamus Deane, B.A. (1961) is teaching with the Christian Brothers in Derry.

Misses Pauline Elkins, B.A., Brenda McEntee, B.A., Claire Agnew, B.A., Maire O'Boyle B.A., and Eileen Cassidy, B.A., have joined the staff of St. Dominic's, Belfast.

Mrs. Kathleen Morgan, B.Sc., is teaching in Mount St. Lourdes, Enniskillen.

Muredach Dynan, B.Sc. (1960) has been appointed to the staff of St. Joseph's Training College.

Miss Moira Mullan, B.A., has been appointed to St. Joseph's Intermediate School, Coleraine.

Desmond Donovan, B.Sc.(Econ.) 1959) has returned to Nigeria for a second term of two years.

Miss Anne Barry, B.A., has been appointed to Donaghmore Convent.

Michael O'Reilly, B.Sc. (1960), Bangor, has gone to Manchester University for three years for further research.

Miss Alice J. McBride, B.A., has been appointed to the new Intermediate School in Draperstown.

Alan Comerton, LL.B. (1960) has been awarded a scholarship for post-graduate study in Pensylvania by the Society of Friendly Sons of St. Patrick.

Miss Mary Kelly, B.A. Portstewart, has returned to Benin City to teach.

Gerard Burns, M.B. (1956) has been awarded his F.R.C.S.

Michael Clarke, B.Sc. (1956) is teaching in St. Patrick's, Barnageeha.

---

3 : *Heaney Group Sheets*

AFTER GRADUATING FROM Queen's University Belfast in 1961, Heaney attended St. Joseph's College of Education, Andersontown, Belfast where he earned a diploma in teaching and did his practice teaching at St. Thomas's Secondary Intermediate School, Belfast. In 1963 he was appointed as a Lecturer at St. Joseph's College of Education. It was at this time that he met Philip Hobsbaum, who had recently arrived from London to teach at Queen's University Belfast. Hobsbaum was a poet and anthologist/editor who had organized poetry workshops first in Cambridge in 1955 and then in London. He quickly did the same in Belfast. Participation in the workshop was overseen by Hobsbaum and was competitive. The original members of The Group poetry workshop in addition to Heaney were Michael Longley, Edna Longley, James Simmons, Stewart Parker, Joan Newmann, and Bernard MacLaverty. Heaney had published a glowing review in *Hibernia* (September 1963) of *A Group Anthology*, edited by Edward Lucie-Smith and Philip Hobsbaum in which he acknowledged the importance of such groups to "beginners," who would "benefit" from the

OVERLEAF: *Belfast Group Sheets*, circa 1965, untitled, mimeographed selection of poems beginning with "The Diviner" by Seamus Heaney and prepared for The Group, a gathering of Belfast poets. 21.5 × 33 cm.

THE DIVINER

Cut from the green hedge a forked hazel stick
That he held tight by the arms of the V:
Circling the terrain, hunting the pluck
Of water, nervous, but professionally

Unfussed.   The pluck came sharp as a sting.
The rod jerked down with precise convulsions,
Spring water suddenly broadcasting
Through a green aerial its secret stations.

The bystanders would ask to have a try.
He handed them the rod without a word.
It lay dead in their grasp till nonchalantly
He gripped expectant wrists.   The hazel stirred.

                              Seamus Heaney

GRAVITIES

High-riding kites appear to range quite freely
Though reined by strings, strict and invisible.
The pigeon that deserts you suddenly
Is heading home, instinctively faithful.

Lovers with barrages of hot insult
Often cut off their nose to spite their face,
Endure a hopeless day, declare their guilt,
Re-enter the native port of their embrace.

Blinding in Paris, for his party-piece
Joyce named the shops along O'Connell Street
And on Iona Colmcille sought ease
By wearing Irish mould next to his feet.

                              Seamus Heaney

ANCESTRAL PHOTOGRAPH

Jaws puff round and solid as a turnip,
Dead eyes are statue's and the upper lip
Bullies the heavy mouth down to a droop.
A bowler suggests the stage Irishman -
Whose look has two parts scorn, two parts dead pan -
His silver watch chain girds him like a hoop.

My father's uncle, from whom he learnt the trade,
Long fixed in sepia tints, begins to fade
And must come down.   Now on the bedroom wall
There is a faded patch where he has been
As if a bandage had been ripped from skin,
Empty plaque to a house's rise and fall.

Twenty years ago I herded cattle
Into pens or held them against a wall
Until my father won at arguing
His own price on a crowd of cattlemen
Who handled rumps, groped teats, stood, paused and then
Bought a round of drinks to clinch the bargain.

                              Contd.../

"criticism of established" poets. In the absence of MFA programs. The Group offered young poets like Heaney an "easier [way] to meet audiences." In preparation for each workshop the poets would compile a few pages of poems in progress to be circulated among the members. For most group sessions the poets distributed only copies of their own poems (as is the case with the Smiths' Group Sheets); however, on a few occasions poems by three or more members were copied and stapled together for circulation. There are differing opinions on how convivial or contentious this process was. Regardless of how one views the dynamics, The Group was an important part of the development of the private poet in the public arena.

4 : *Eleven Poems*

ELEVEN POEMS was Seamus Heaney's first separately published work. Published November 2, 1965, at "Two shillings and six pence each," informed estimates put the initial print run at one thousand copies. For many years dealers did not realize that two of the three first editions looked very similar and often listed the second issue as the true first. The first edition, first issue has a nine-point sun symbol in purple on the front cover, which also serves as the title page. This issue was printed on cream laid paper. The sun symbol device was used as the logo for the 1965 Belfast Festival. The first edition, second issue, was published in 1966. This edition is approximately the same size, with the same binding and font as the true first, but the cover has a slightly redrawn ten-point sun in a blackish purple. The issue was printed on

Eleven Poems Festival Publications Queen's University of Belfast: white cover, purple nine-pointed star (Heaney's first book, first edition, first issue) 1965, 13 × 20.5 cm; white cover, black ten-pointed star (second state) 1966, 12.5 × 20 cm; green cover (third state) 1966/1967, 14.5 × 21 cm.

white wove paper. The publication was part of a series of poetry pamphlets planned for publication by Queen's University Belfast. The front cover of the first edition, third issue carries the design of the drum and trumpet, which is the logo for the 1966 Festival. The first edition, third issue has an eclectic publishing presence with copies appearing in different sizes, with differing orders of poems, and a variety of typographical errors on the back cover. At least one copy has the poems of another poet between the Heaney covers. All of the poems except one were collected in Heaney's first trade edition, *Death of a Naturalist* (Faber, 1966).

5 : Death of a Naturalist

Death of a Naturalist,
Faber and Faber, 1966,
green cloth with orange
and tan dust jacket,
14 × 21.5 cm.

BY THE TIME Seamus Heaney published his first collection of poems, *Death of a Naturalist* in May of 1966, over sixty of his poems, essays, and reviews had appeared in various periodicals and anthologies in Northern Ireland, Ireland, and England. Heaney had been searching for a publisher for his first collection and had sent the famous Irish publishing house Dolmen Press a noticeably different collection of poems — *Advancements of Learning* — than what eventually appeared as *Death of a Naturalist* published in London by Faber. Dolmen Press turned down the book and the rest is history. The dust jacket of the first edition of *Death of a Naturalist* is typical of the Faber minimalist, font heavy design of the period. The collection's title, taken from the poem "Death of a Naturalist," first appeared in *Poetry Ireland* in 1965 as "End of a Naturalist." The general themes of the book are captured in the title: childhood memories of Ulster farm life, loss of innocence, the birth of the poet, the break with his family's past, negotiating the world of Catholic–Protestant sectarian tensions, and his courtship and marriage to Marie Devlin. The first poem in the volume, "Digging," is amazingly still one of his most famous. The closing lines, "Between my finger and my thumb / The squat pen rests. / I'll dig with it," announce his poetic method and preoccupations — going down into the past, land, and language. Critics responded for the most part positively to Heaney's concrete language and formal writing style, and *Death of a Naturalist* won the 1966 Eric Gregory Award, which is given by the Society of Authors (UK) to British poets under thirty (Heaney was twenty-seven when his first book appeared). In 1967 the book received the Cholmondeley Award also given by the Society of Authors (UK) for distinguished works of poetry. Faber has no record of the number of *Death of a Naturalist* copies printed.

6 : The Island People

THE 1968 PAMPHLET *The Island People* must be one of the most overlooked of Heaney's publications. Appearing as "A3" in the Heaney bibliography, it occupies a place of distinction. Ironically, *The Island People* was initially delegated to section "D"— Contributions to Exhibition Catalogues and Programmes — until one of the book's final drafts. Grolier Club member and primary consultant to the Heaney bibliography, Jim O'Halloran argued for years that it was an "A" item while I thought that it belonged with the other BBC programs and musical performance materials. The turning point came when we decided to include *Dairy of One Who Vanished* (1999) in Section "A." This was a version of a song cycle from the Czech of Leoš Janáčk. The lyrics and poems that appear in *The Island People* are to be found nowhere else in Heaney's publications. While there are numerous published poems and translations that were never collected in a single Heaney volume, the poet was not averse to revising for collection poems from the "D" items. There are also the publications like *Stations* (1975) and the Middle English translation *The Names of the Hare* (1982), which remained discreet publications for decades before appearing in this case in *Opened Ground* (1999). *The Island People* contains the only song lyrics written by Heaney.

The Island People, British Broadcasting Corporation, summer 1968, an Irish sequence of poetry by Seamus Heaney and music by Gerard Victory, white, blue, and black cover, 17.5 × 23.5 cm.

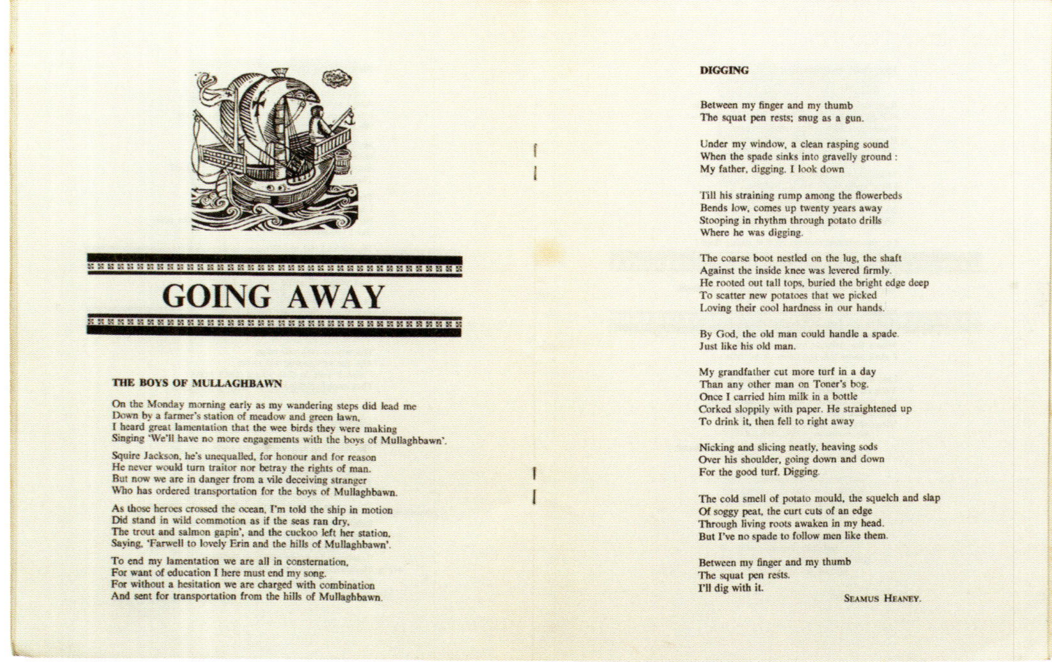

GOING AWAY

THE BOYS OF MULLAGHBAWN

On the Monday morning early as my wandering steps did lead me
Down by a farmer's station of meadow and green lawn,
I heard great lamentation that the wee birds they were making
Singing 'We'll have no more engagements with the boys of Mullaghbawn'.

Squire Jackson, he's unequalled, for honour and for reason
He never would turn traitor nor betray the rights of man.
But now we are in danger from a vile deceiving stranger
Who has ordered transportation for the boys of Mullaghbawn.

As those heroes crossed the ocean, I'm told the ship in motion
Did stand in wild commotion as if the seas ran dry,
The trout and salmon gapin', and the cuckoo left her station,
Saying, 'Farwell to lovely Erin and the hills of Mullaghbawn'.

To end my lamentation we are all in consternation,
For want of education I here must end my song.
For without a hesitation we are charged with combination
And sent for transportation from the hills of Mullaghbawn.

DIGGING

Between my finger and my thumb
The squat pen rests; snug as a gun.

Under my window, a clean rasping sound
When the spade sinks into gravelly ground :
My father, digging. I look down

Till his straining rump among the flowerbeds
Bends low, comes up twenty years away
Stooping in rhythm through potato drills
Where he was digging.

The coarse boot nestled on the lug, the shaft
Against the inside knee was levered firmly.
He rooted out tall tops, buried the bright edge deep
To scatter new potatoes that we picked
Loving their cool hardness in our hands.

By God, the old man could handle a spade.
Just like his old man.

My grandfather cut more turf in a day
Than any other man on Toner's bog.
Once I carried him milk in a bottle
Corked sloppily with paper. He straightened up
To drink it, then fell to right away

Nicking and slicing neatly, heaving sods
Over his shoulder, going down and down
For the good turf. Digging.

The cold smell of potato mould, the squelch and slap
Of soggy peat, the curt cuts of an edge
Through living roots awaken in my head.
But I've no spade to follow men like them.

Between my finger and my thumb
The squat pen rests.
I'll dig with it.

SEAMUS HEANEY.

Room to Rhyme, Arts Council of Northern Ireland, 1968, red paper cover, 18 × 23 cm.

PUBLISHED IN 1968 by the Arts Council of Northern Ireland, *Room to Rhyme* served as the program for community performances by Seamus Heaney, fellow Belfast poet Michael Longley, and the folk singer and filmmaker David Hammond. The group, comprised of artists from both Protestant and Catholic backgrounds, represented an alternative to the growing schism between the two communities. Heaney and Longley would read their poems and Hammond would perform songs associated with both heritages. The pamphlet contains nine poems by Heaney, three of which were previously uncollected. Of those three, "Requiem for the Croppies," first published in the Summer 1966 issue of *Dublin Magazine*, is one of Heaney's most famous examinations of the resilience of the Irish rebel spirit. The poem was written during the fiftieth anniversary year of the 1916 Easter Rising; however, Heaney chose to recognize the seeds of that rebellion in the 1798 battle at Vinegar Hill, County Wexford. Heaney explains the origins of the title *Room to Rhyme* in the 2004 University of Dundee publication of *Room to Rhyme*, which is the text of the university's "Greatest Minds Lecture" given by the poet in July of 2003. After quoting "Room, room, my gallant boys, / And give us room to rhyme," he says: "These are the opening lines of a mummers' play that used to be performed locally when I was a youngster in County Derry."

8 : *A Lough Neagh Sequence*

WHILE SEAMUS HEANEY has a long list of limited edition publications, it all began with *A Lough Neagh Sequence*, which was published by the Phoenix Pamphlet Poets Press in January 1969. The first 50 copies of an edition of 1,000 were signed by the author on the title page. The remaining 950 are issued in stapled white card covers. "A Lough Neagh Sequence" was first published in the Winter 1967 issue of *University Review* (Dublin) and collected with revisions in *Door into the Dark* (1969). The eel, which spends part of its life on land and the other in water, appears in many of Heaney's poems as a metaphor for the amphibious nature of the poet who lives in his imagination and in the world. The tightly woven interlacing image of the cover links the eels to the ancient zoomorphic work of the Irish illuminated manuscripts, while the dedication "For the Fishermen" and quotes from *The Fishes of Great Britain and Ireland* connect it to the modern world of the eel industry on Lough Neagh — the lake not far from Heaney's childhood home and near the home place of his wife, Marie Devlin. The magazine *Phoenix*

Seamus Heaney was born in 1939 and grew up on a farm in County Derry, Northern Ireland. He was educated at St. Columb's College, Derry, and at Queen's University, Belfast, where he is now a lecturer in the English Department. He has also done school and College of Education teaching. He is married with two children. His first collection, 'Death of a Naturalist' (Faber, 1966) was given the Cholmondeley Award for Poets in 1967 and a Somerset Maugham Award in 1968. 'A Lough Neagh Sequence' forms part of 'Door Into The Dark', a new collection of poems by Seamus Heaney to be published by Faber & Faber in mid-1969. These poems are included in a selection of his own work read by the poet on a record, 'The Northern Muse' (Claddagh Records, Dublin); another selection is to be found on Record Nine of 'The Poet Speaks' series (Argo).

A Lough Neagh Sequence, Phoenix Pamphlet Poets Press, January 1969, 50 signed copies in an edition of 1,000, green cloth boards, white dust jacket, 12.5 × 20 cm. The back photograph shows the smoking Heaney, young, urban, and confident.

(Belfast, North Ireland) had published several of Heaney's poems in 1967, and its editor Harry Chambers had launched the Phoenix Pamphlet Poets Press in 1968 with an emphasis on emerging poets.

9 : *A Boy Driving His Father to Confession*

A Boy Driving His Father to Confession, The Sceptre Press, 1970, Farnham, Surrey, 150 copies, 50 signed by author, white paper cover, 12.5 × 20.5 cm.

SEAMUS HEANEY'S ACCESS TO and interest in small presses and limited editions were the result of his appreciation for the look of the book (or broadside) and the dynamics of literary production in general. These publishers offered Heaney the intimacy of the single poem or small collection and the pleasure of working one-on-one with the artistic design. *A Boy Driving His Father to Confession* was published in December 1970 by Sceptre Press, Farnham, Surrey, in an edition of 150 numbered copies; 1–50 are signed by the poet. In addition, five copies numbered i–v were bound in dark red leather and signed by the poet and the publisher, Martin Booth. The 150 copies, which appear with stapled white card covers, sold for £0.25, and the leather bound copies sold for £2.10. The Heaney bibliography entry for this edition of *A Boy Driving His Father to Confession* contains the note "[not seen]." At Sceptre Press Martin Booth also published a slim volume by Ted Hughes, *A Crow Hymn* (1970). "A Boy Driving His Father to Confession" first appeared in the March 1967 issue of *Phoenix* and is reprinted here in the limited edition with revisions. The poem has never appeared in a trade edition of Heaney's poetry, only in the limited edition collection *Poems and a Memoir* (1982).

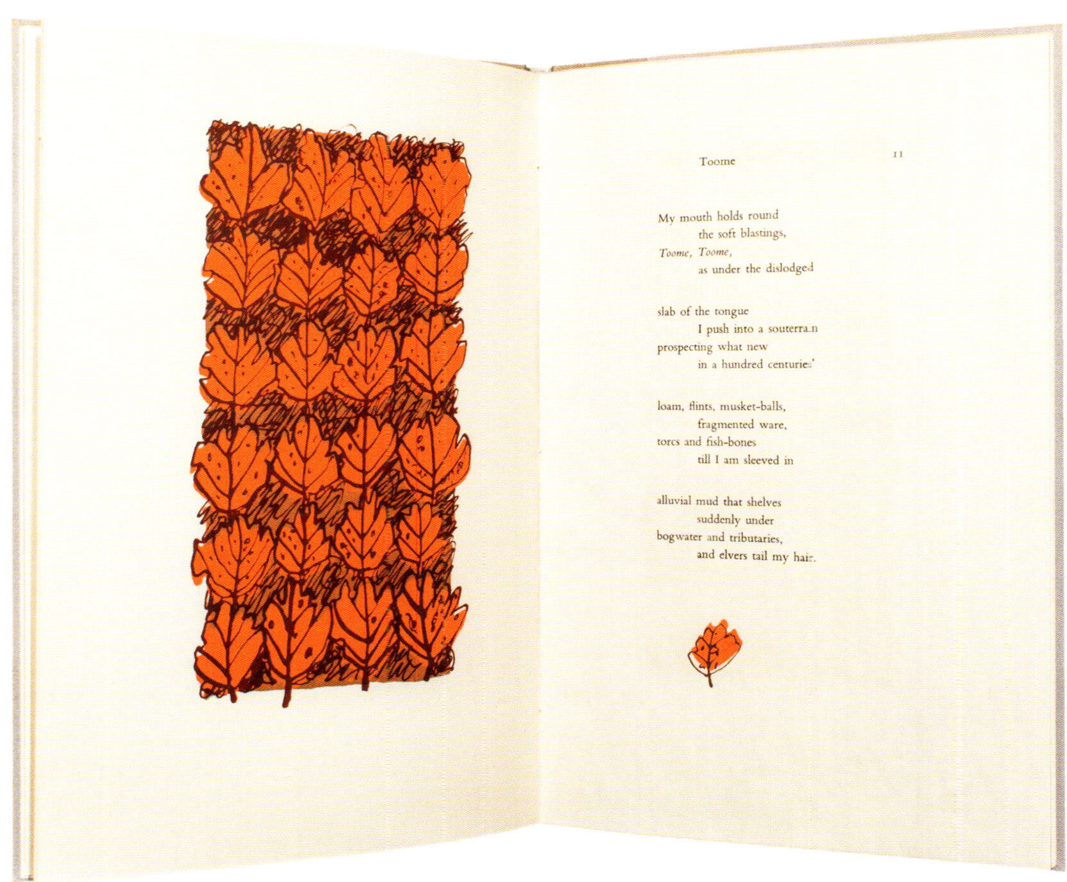

10 : *Toome*

SEAMUS HEANEY'S FRIEND, fellow Field Day Theatre director, and Irish playwright Brian Friel brings to life in his play *Translations* (1980) the moment in Irish history when the British Government attempted in the 1833 Ordinance Survey to anglicize all of the features of the Irish landscape — cities, towns, villages, crossroads, roads; mountains, valleys, lakes, rivers, streams; and sacred places and places marked by history and myth. This attempted linguistic conquest was just the logical extension of the military conquest, conquests that only partially succeeded. Much of Heaney's work explores the way in which place names, Irish place names, are used and pronounced to reinforce the political divisions and to subvert them. In Heaney's work, there is a direct connection between the land and the language as presented in some of his most important early poems, such as "Broagh," "Anahorish," and "Toome."

Toome, published by the National College of Art and Design in 1980, in an edition of 15 hand-numbered copies dated and signed

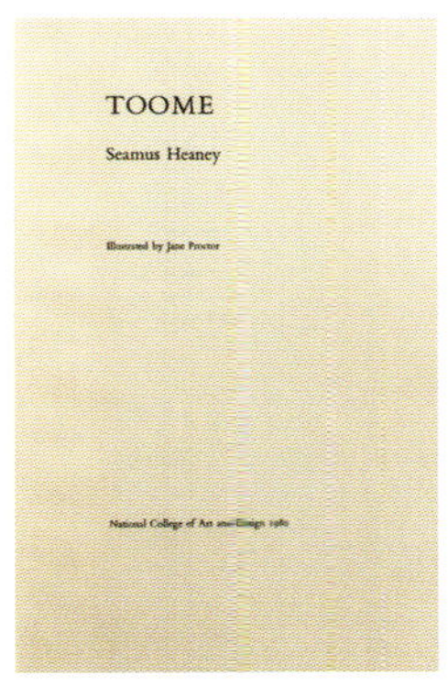

Toome, National College of Art and Design, Dublin, October 1980, illustrated by Jane Proctor, gray boards, 15 numbered copies signed by artist and many signed later by author on request, 18 × 28 cm.

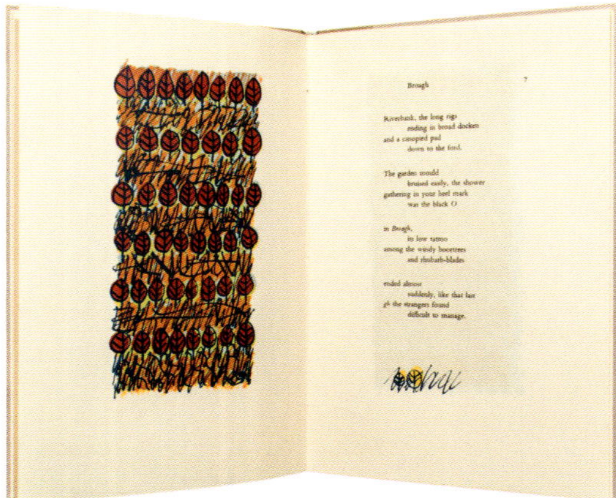

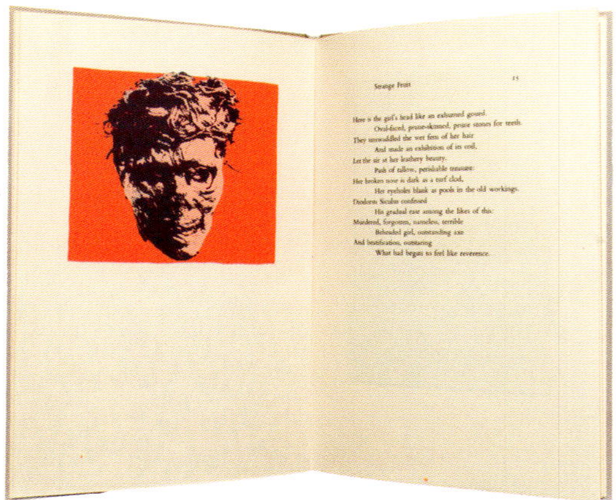

by the illustrator Jane Proctor, brings together these land-language poems in a small but powerful selection. Since all of the poems in *Toome* had been previously published, it seems as if the *Toome* project had been initiated by Proctor who had been working on a series of silkscreen posters in 1980 for events for Irish poets Harry Clifton and John Ennis. In addition, the poet did not sign all of the copies even though the description of *Toome* in *Seamus Heaney: A Bibliography 1959–2003* says that he did. It appears that all of the copies that the editors saw were signed after the 1980 publishing date since some copies were sold without Heaney's signature. Still, in terms of collecting between boards previously published Heaney poems for a very small print run, *Toome* joins *Four Poems* (twelve copies) as the rarest of the rare.

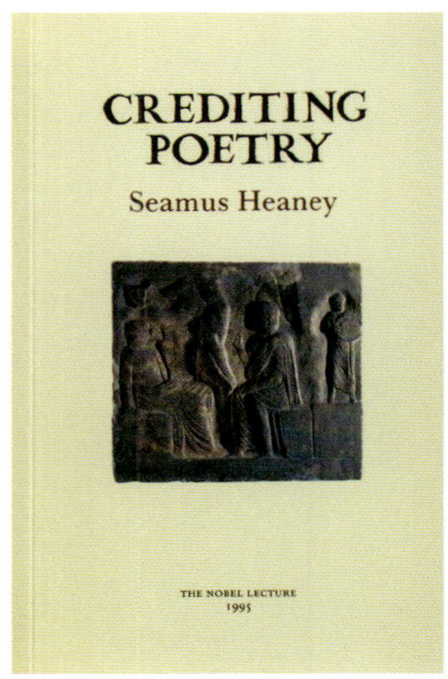  

11 : *Crediting Poetry*

S EAMUS AND MARIE HEANEY were traveling with friends in Greece in October 1995. October is "Nobel Month," and for who knows how long Heaney had been short-listed for the Nobel Prize in Literature. So for obvious reasons it was much more relaxing for the poet to be away from Dublin's optimistic journalists during this time of the year. Yet, it was in October of 1995 that Heaney received the call in Greece informing him that he had been awarded the Nobel Prize and asking if he would accept it. The Nobel Selection Committee cannot announce the name of the winner until they accept — some have declined the award. Since the Nobel Prize in Literature requires an acceptance speech, Heaney responded with *Crediting Poetry*. The poet had just survived over two decades of Post-Structuralist and Deconstructionist criticism, which had tried to kill the author and devaluate poetry. So in *Crediting Poetry*, Heaney credits poetry for its ability to bring balance to our lives by not letting the "murderous" overshadow the "marvelous," and for being a fundamental source and continuance of our essential human values.

The text of Seamus Heaney's lecture was printed and circulated in unbound sheets in Stockholm by the Nobel Foundation/Swedish Academy on the day of the awards ceremony. Following this down home method of distribution, *Crediting Poetry* appears in three trade editions. The first edition was published by Gallery Books on December 12, 1995; Heaney obviously wanted an Irish publisher to launch the book in Ireland. The Gallery edition has an image of a stone relief on the front cover. Heaney connects in this image his

Crediting Poetry: The Nobel Lecture, 1995, delivered before the Swedish Academy on December 7, 1995: Gallery Books first issue, 1995, yellow paper card covers, 14 × 21.5 cm: Privately printed for Faber, 1996, by Smith Settle, Otley, West Yorkshire, 500 signed copies, blue paper cover with green dust jacket, 13.5 × 21.5 cm; FSG, 1996, beige paper covered boards with multi-colored dust jacket, 12 × 19 cm.

Images for jacket designs are reused on two occasions. Faber's *The Spirit Level* adopts the main image of three skeps from FSG's *Crediting Poetry* (see previous page). FSG's *The Spirit Level*, in contrast, features a photograph of a spirit level. Faber's *District and Circle* (2006) incorporates a detail from *North* (1975).

trip to Greece, the Greek allusions in his earliest work ("Personal Helicon"), and the mythic sources that have provided a potent way for the poet to understand and discuss the place of poetry in the world and the role of the poet in our lives. The first English edition of *Crediting Poetry* was published by Faber in 1996 in an edition of 500 copies and circulated privately. Unlike the understated and stately olive green dust jacket of the Faber edition, upon which one finds only the poet's name and the essay title, the first American edition published by Farrar, Straus and Giroux (FSG) appears between boards and has an iconic image from the Ashmole Bestiary on the front and back covers. This image is of three lines of bees going into three medieval beehives — the honey bee being the archetypal creature of social organization and the hive being the source of all things sweet.

Interestingly, this image from the Ashmole Bestiary on the cover of *Crediting Poetry* also appears in a slightly different iteration on the cover of the Faber first editions in boards and in wrappers of *The Spirit Level*, also published in 1996. This is the only time a cover image appears twice on separate Heaney trade publications, with the notable exceptions *North* (1972) and *District and Circle* (2006). On the paperback covers of the Faber first edition in wrappers of *District and Circle* the publishers re-appropriate a section from the 1974 portrait of Heaney by Edward McGuire that appears on the back cover of *North*. The painting is of Heaney at a desk with dense foliage behind him out of which appear the heads of birds. One of these birds dominates the front cover of *District and Circle*, which includes the poem, "The Blackbird of Glanmore." However as Heaney has mentioned, the bird does not even look like a blackbird — the attempt at a literal transposition or suggestion of some kind of prescience on the part of the publisher just does not fly here, unlike the promising cross pollination of *Crediting Poetry* and *The Spirit Level*.

12 : *The Government of the Tongue, The Redress of Poetry*

SEAMUS HEANEY WAS not only the most accomplished reader of his own poetry, he was also the most accomplished deliverer of his own ideas. The poet was an orator of the first degree. Thus it was appropriate that his first official teaching position at Harvard was as the Bolyston Professor of Rhetoric and Oratory (a distinguished position that has evolved to accommodate mostly poets of note not possessing an earned doctorate). Of course, his critical acumen (in addition to his poetic accomplishments) had earned him numerous honorary doctorates, invitations to deliver a variety of named lectures, and more involved academic commitments, such as the Oxford Professor of Poetry and the Richard Ellmann Memorial Lectures, published as *The Place of Writing*, presented at Emory University, and organized by Grolier Club member Ron Schuchard. In 2004 his talents were recognized, materializing like Yeats's Cuchullain in the General Post Office, when Queen's University Belfast established the Seamus Heaney Centre for Poetry. Despite his concern that the writing of the critical prose might compromise the writing of the poetry, he published four major volumes of criticism: *Preoccupations: Selected Prose 1968–1978* (1980); *The Government of the Tongue: The 1986 T. S. Eliot Memorial Lectures and Other Critical Writings* (1988); *The Redress of Poetry: Oxford Lectures* (1995); and *Finders Keepers: Selected Prose 1971–2001* (2002).

The English and American first editions of the prose collections reflect the same publishing and design differences between Faber

The Place of Writing, Scholars Press, Emory University, 1989, 3,000 copies, 60 numbered and signed by the author (numbers 1–30 not for sale), navy cloth with green dust jacket, with photo of Ellmann and Heaney, 14 × 21.5 cm.

Preoccupations: Selected Prose 1968–1978, FSG, 1980.

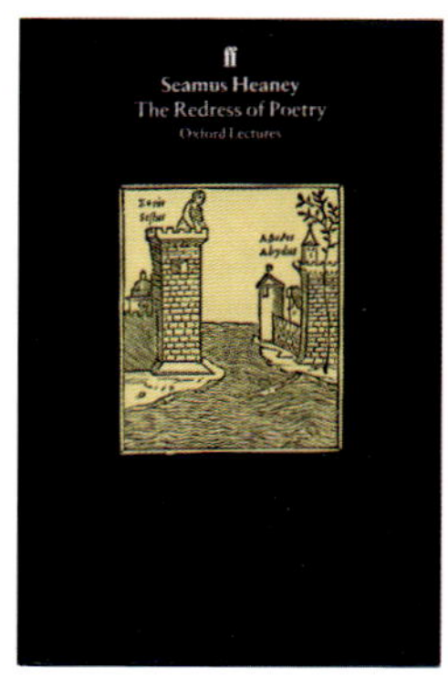

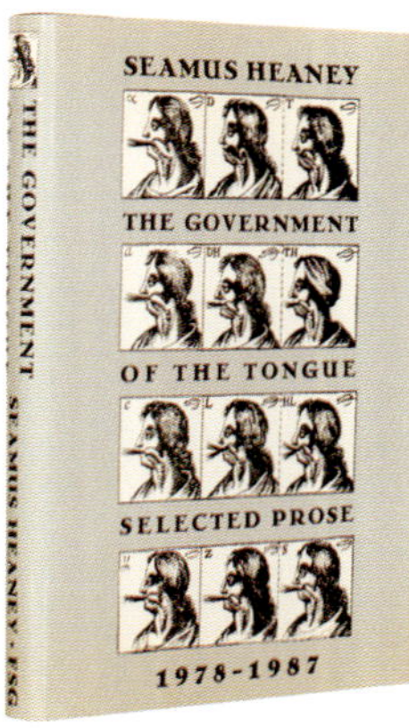

The Redress of Poetry and The Government of the Tongue dust jackets demonstrating the different design approaches between the publishers Faber and FSG.

and Faber and Farrar, Straus and Giroux that informed the books of Heaney's poetry—Faber is more text heavy, design light, and FSG is more image conscious and market oriented. However, while the first Faber and FSG editions of *Preoccupations* resembled each other in terms of their cover designs, by the time *The Government of the Tongue* appeared, the English and American publishers were taking different approaches to their audiences. The Faber first edition of *The Government of the Tongue* includes on the cover the subtitle: *The 1986 T. S Eliot Memorial Lectures and Other Critical Writings*; the subtitle does not appear in or on the American FSG first edition. Both publishers take the same approach to *The Redress of Poetry: Oxford Lectures*, where the subtitle *Oxford Lectures* does not appear on or in the FSG first edition.

One can only surmise the various reasons for the absence of the subtitles. The differences that appear in the English and American first editions of Heaney's *Selected Poems* — Faber's *Selected Poems 1965–1975* (1980) and FSG's *Poems 1965–1975* (1980) — provided the publishers a marketing distinction. Not using "Selected Poems" in the FSG title allowed the poet to title his next FSG selected poems *Selected Poems: 1966–1987*, and the Faber collection became *New Selected Poems 1966–1987* (1990). This method of distinguishing between the English and American editions continues in *Opened Ground* (1998). The English edition subtitle reads: *Poems 1966–1996*; the American subtitle reads: *Selected Poems 1966–1996*. These seemingly minor differences between the English and American first editions of collections of Heaney's selected work in which the prose and poems are the same reflect a major shift in the understanding of the modes of literary production and the mechanizations of marketing a global poet.

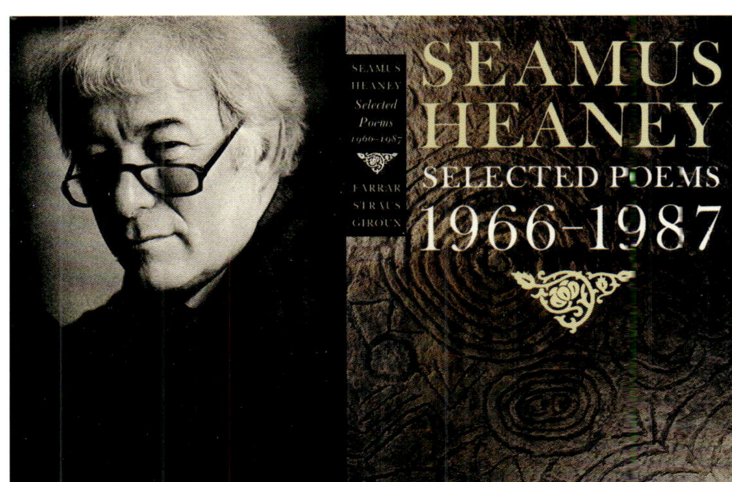

Faber dust jackets and covers on left and FSG's on right illustrate the publishers' use of different titles for the same book of poems gathered as selections. OPPOSITE PAGE: The publishers used different subtitles for American and British audiences.

The Gravel Walks, printed by Richard Murdoch at Shadowy Waters Press, Winston-Salem, North Carolina, March 14, 1992, for Lenoir-Rhyne College (now University), Hickory, North Carolina, 175 copies, gray and orange marbled cover, 13.5 × 14.5 cm.

OPPOSITE: Intended by Heaney to be a conventional character space, the large white spaces within the lines of the poem are an accurate reflection of his original text as delivered to the printer. No proofs were sent. Heaney first saw the printed poem while reveling with friends and said, "I like the spacing."

13 : *The Gravel Walks, A Keen for the Coins*

CELEBRATING SEAMUS HEANEY'S 1992 and 2003 visits to Lenoir-Rhyne University in Hickory, North Carolina, the limited editions *The Gravel Walks* and *A Keen for the Coins* represent some of the finest small press publications produced for a campus event and are connected to earlier Heaney limited editions marking similar visits at other institutions by the poet. *The Gravel Walks* was published by Lenoir-Rhyne College (now University) and printed by Shadowy Waters Press of Winston-Salem, North Carolina. The poem was distributed to the participants of the 1992 American Conference for Irish Studies Southern Regional Conference hosted by the college and appeared in two editions: a limited numbered edition of 175 copies and a special edition lettered A–Z and signed by the author. Two other iterations of the publication exist: 10 "Artists Copies" and 10 unfolded, unbound sheets, all numbered and signed by the author. Through this series of printing formats it is as if one is watching the printing process in reverse

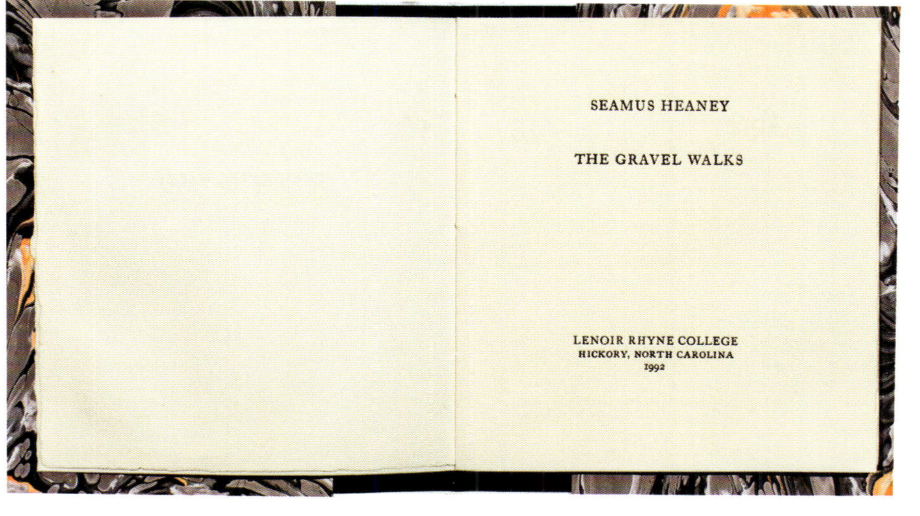

SEAMUS HEANEY

THE GRAVEL WALKS

LENOIR RHYNE COLLEGE
HICKORY, NORTH CAROLINA
1992

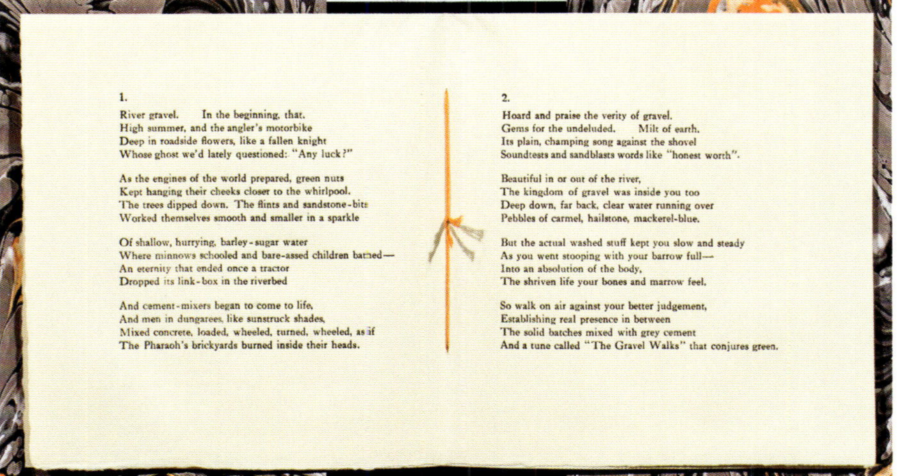

1.

River gravel.   In the beginning, that.
High summer, and the angler's motorbike
Deep in roadside flowers, like a fallen knight
Whose ghost we'd lately questioned: "Any luck?"

As the engines of the world prepared, green nuts
Kept hanging their cheeks closer to the whirlpool.
The trees dipped down. The flints and sandstone-bits
Worked themselves smooth and smaller in a sparkle

Of shallow, hurrying, barley-sugar water
Where minnows schooled and bare-assed children bathed—
An eternity that ended once a tractor
Dropped its link-box in the riverbed

And cement-mixers began to come to life,
And men in dungarees, like sunstruck shades,
Mixed concrete, loaded, wheeled, turned, wheeled, as if
The Pharaoh's brickyards burned inside their heads.

2.

Hoard and praise the verity of gravel.
Gems for the undeluded.   Milt of earth.
Its plain, champing song against the shovel
Soundtests and sandblasts words like "honest worth".

Beautiful in or out of the river,
The kingdom of gravel was inside you too
Deep down, far back, clear water running over
Pebbles of carmel, hailstone, mackerel-blue.

But the actual washed stuff kept you slow and steady
As you went stooping with your barrow full—
Into an absolution of the body,
The shriven life your bones and marrow feel.

So walk on air against your better judgement,
Establishing real presence in between
The solid batches mixed with grey cement
And a tune called "The Gravel Walks" that conjures green.

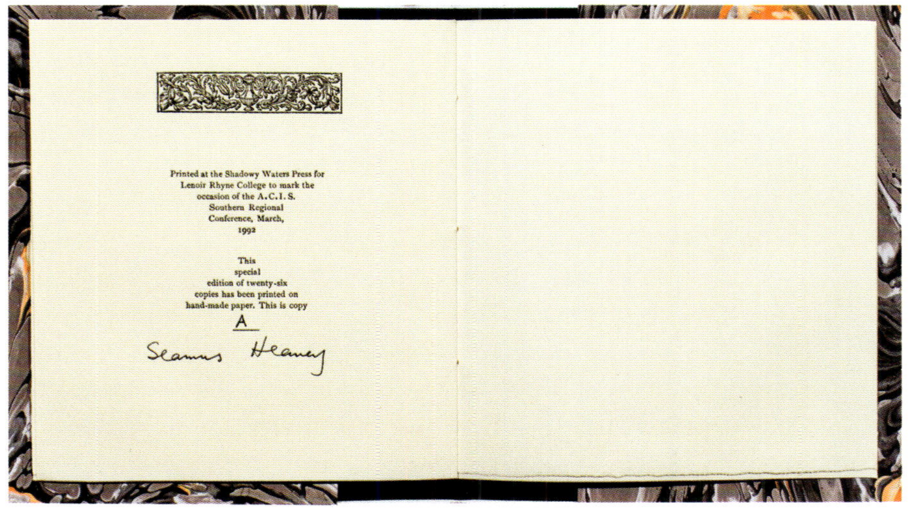

Printed at the Shadowy Waters Press for
Lenoir Rhyne College to mark the
occasion of the A.C.I.S.
Southern Regional
Conference, March,
1992

This
special
edition of twenty-six
copies has been printed on
hand-made paper. This is copy
A

Seamus Heaney

A Keen for the Coins, printed by Richard Murdoch at Shadowy Waters Press, Winston-Salem, North Carolina, 2002, for Lenoir-Rhyne College (now University), Hickory, North Carolina, gilded paper cover, 100 copies with a lettered edition of 26, some signed by the author, 12.5 × 12.5 cm.

from the unfolded and unbound sheets, to what are essentially artist's proofs, to the lettered edition, to the limited edition.

Indicative of Heaney's expansive publishing practices and generosity from another perspective, the Lenoir-Rhyne *The Gravel Walks* is the poem's first separate publication; however, the poem also appeared in 1992 in *The Poetry Book Society Anthology 3* and in the summer issue of *The Thinker Review* (Louisville, Kentucky). One of the editors of *The Thinker Review*, Ron Whitehead, attended the Lenoir-Rhyne conference where he met Heaney and later published two poster poems of Heaney's work, *A Dog Was Crying in Wicklow Also* and *The Clay Pipes*. So, one conference produced four occasional publications. *The Gravel Walks* was later collected with revisions in

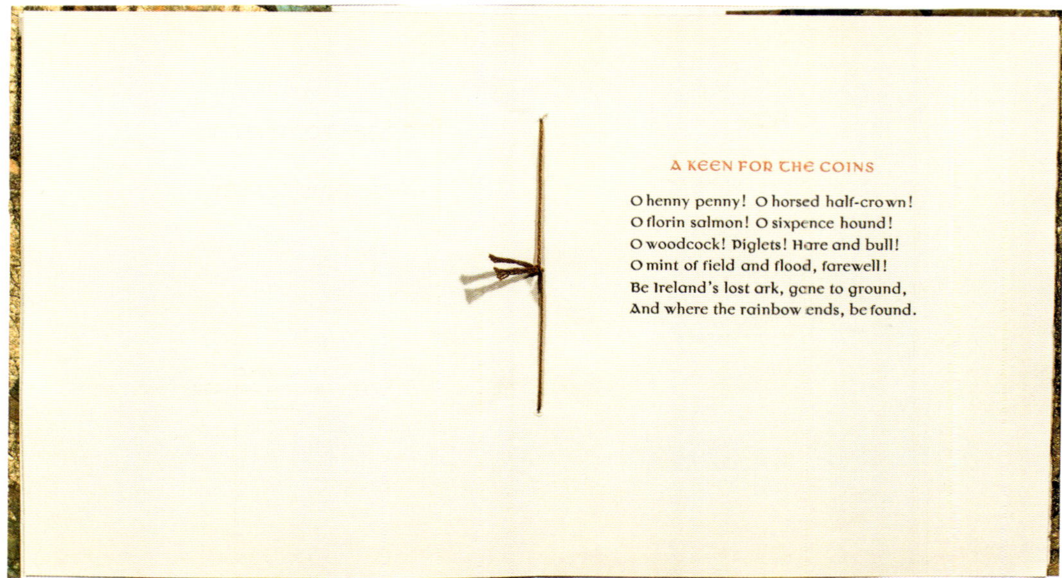

The Spirit Level. The poem takes its title from a famous Irish reel, but the lines are pure Heaney.

Richard Murdoch printed both editions of *The Gravel Walks* at Shadowy Waters Press. Murdoch has a long history of printing limited editions of Heaney poems. Before he printed the first and limited editions of *The Sounds of Rain* for Emory University's inaugural Richard Ellmann Memorial Lecture in 1988, Murdoch had printed *Dánta Idir Ghaeilge Agus Bhéarla* for the America Conference for Irish Studies annual meeting in 1984 at Wake Forest University in Winston-Salem, North Carolina, where he was employed by the university library, and for the Wake Forest University Press. Wake Forest University Press worked in collaboration with Gallery Press, County Meath, Ireland, for many years publishing established and emerging Irish poets — but never any works by Heaney. Murdoch was also the printer of the first separate edition and lettered edition of *A Keen for the Coins*, which was published to mark the opening of *Seamus Heaney's Ars Poetica* — an exhibition of rare publications and manuscripts at the Hickory Museum of Art, in Hickory, North Carolina, and curated by Rand Brandes. The poem "A Keen for the Coins" marks the end of the use of the Irish currency designed for the new Irish Republic in the late 1920s and the adoption of the euro on January 1, 2002. The front wrapper of the first separate edition is embossed with the reverse of a 1928 Irish coin. Murdoch was known for his fine design, materials, craftsmanship, and attention to detail. These limited editions were handsewn by Murdoch himself occasionally in his car parked outside the reading venue.

The Sounds of Rain, published in memory of Richard Ellmann and printed by Richard Murdoch at Shadowy Waters Press, Winston-Salem, North Carolina, 1988, for Emory University's inaugural Richard Ellmann Memorial Lectures.

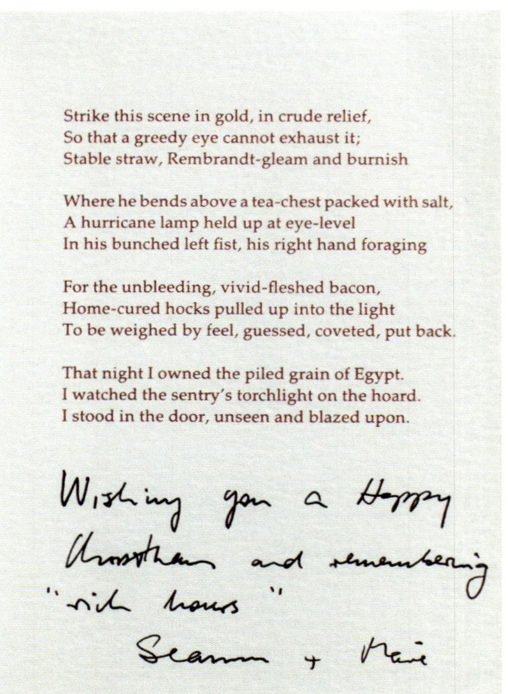

A Rich Hour,
printed by Peter
Fallon, 1988,
Christmas card
inscribed to
Charles Monteith,
14.5 × 21 cm
folded.

14 : *Christmas Cards*

IN ITS USE of a section identified as "AA: Broadsides and Cards," *Seamus Heaney: A Bibliography 1959–2003* diverges from most descriptive bibliographies Most bibliographies would include the author's broadsides and cards that appear as first editions or first separate publications as "A" items along with "Books and Pamphlets" or even place them in the ephemera section. However, dividing section "A" into two sub-sections captures Heaney's complex publishing history. In addition, this division preserves the prominence of the trade editions while acknowledging the unique importance of the privately printed "AA" items in Heaney's publishing life. Of these privately printed items are a series of Christmas cards containing short poems and, occasionally, translations by the poet.

Heaney began the practice of sending poems to family and friends as Christmas gifts beginning with *Catherine's Poem* published in 1976 and printed in County Wicklow in an edition of 75 copies. The second card, *Christmas Eve*, was privately printed by the author in 1978 in an edition of 125 copies by Peter Fallon (on later cards listed as "Peter Fallon/Gallery Press"). There were 18 privately printed Christmas cards published between 1976 and 2003. Early on, Heaney typically published the Christmas cards in editions of 125 copies; not surprisingly this number grew to 300 copies by the

2000s. The front image on some of the cards, such as *A Rich Hour* and *The Settle Bed*, were drawn by the poet's daughter, Catherine Ann. *The Settle Bed* Christmas card displayed in the exhibition is addressed to Charles Monteith, the editor at Faber who accepted Heaney's first volume, *Death of a Naturalist*, for publication. In the memorial service address for Charles Monteith at St. George's Church, Bloomsbury, on Thursday, September 21, 1995, Heaney states: "I myself had always a special sense of relationship and gratitude to him, since I was the first poet he took on to the Faber list after the death of Eliot." This address was delivered just a few weeks before Heaney received the Nobel Prize.

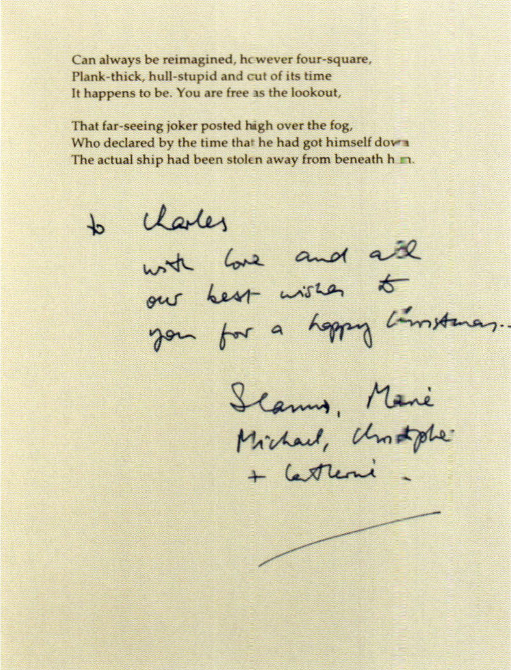

The Settle Bed, Peter Fallon, 1989, Christmas card inscribed to Charles Monteith and hand-corrected by Heaney, illustration by Catherine Ann Heaney, daughter, 15 × 21 cm folded.

The majority of the poems selected by Heaney for the cards have some connection with the holiday, the winter season, or the new year as with *Jesus and the Sparrows* (1996) and *I Sing of a Maiden* (2005). Others are short elegies to the passing of the year and to the dead recently remembered. For example, *Would They Had Stay'd* (1997) laments the passing of three Scottish poets — Norman MacCaig (1910–1996), Sorley MacLean (1911–1996), and George Mackay Brown (1921–1996) — and opens with

"WOULD THEY HAD STAYED"

1

The colour of meadow hay, with its meadow-sweet
And liver-spotted dock leaves, they were there
Before we spotted them, all eyes and evening,
Up to their necks in the meadow.
                                        'Where? I still —'
'There.'
            'Oh yes. Oh God, yes. Lovely.'
                                        And they didn't
Move away.
                    There, like the air on hold.
The step of light on grass, halted mid-light.
Heartbeat and pupil. A match for us. And watching.

2

Norman MacCaig, come forth from the deer of Magdalen,
Those startlers standing still in fritillary land,
Heather-sentries far from the heath. Be fawn
To the redcoat, gallowglass in the Globe,
Tidings of trees that walked and were seen to walk.

ABOVE AND OPPOSITE: *Would They Had Stay'd*, Peter Fallon/The Gallery Press, 1997, Christmas card, 21 × 15 cm folded. Heaney would often notify Brandes, as he does on the back of the card, of forthcoming publications to be included in the bibliography.

LEFT: *Jesus and the Sparrows*, Peter Fallon/The Gallery Press, 1996, Christmas card, 175 copies, 14.5 × 23.5 cm folded.

BOTTOM LEFT: *I Sing of a Maiden*, Peter Fallon/The Gallery Press, 2003, illustration on cover created in 1978 by Catherine Ann Heaney, daughter, at the age of five.

an allusion to the deer, "Time, the deer, is in Hallaig Wood," that appears in Heaney's translation from the Scottish of MacLean's famous poem "Hallaig." "Would They Had Stay'd" first appeared in *Poetry Review*, Winter 1997/1998, and was collected with revisions in *Electric Light* (2001). The poem's title is taken from *Macbeth*, Act 1, Scene III, following the three witches' prophecies that Macbeth shall be king. Macbeth wishes to hear more, saying, "Would they had stay'd…." The poem's title is printed incorrectly on the Christmas card; Heaney corrects the title by hand on the exhibition copy, changing "Stayed" to "Stay'd." The Christmas card publication *Would They Had Stay'd* gives the poem a poignancy that none of the other publications could possess. Few who received this gift could have imagined its true depth.

3

Sorley MacLean. A mirage. A stag on a ridge
In the western desert above the burnt-out tanks.

4

What George Mackay Brown saw was a drinking deer
That glittered by the water. The human soul
In mosaic. Wet celandine and ivy.
Allegory hard as Earl Rognvald's shield
Polished until its undersurface surfaced
Like peat smoke mulling through Byzantium.

And a Happy Christmas to you all — after you do this take-home final… Much love from everyone at Strand Road — Seamus

P.S. Rand, This will appear, slightly revised, in the next issue of Poetry Review, the English magazine.

"Would they had stay'd"
Macbeth, Act I, Scene iii
'The Deer' from Basilica San Clemente, Rome
courtesy of Soprintendenza per i Beni Artistici
and Paul Lawlor OP

———————————

"Would They Had Stayed"
© Seamus Heaney 1997
Privately published for the author
by Peter Fallon/The Gallery Press
Loughcrew · Oldcastle · County Meath · Ireland
Christmas 1997

I N THE EARLY 1980S Seamus Heaney worked with the British poet Ted Hughes on an anthology of poems for children, *The Rattle Bag*. Published in 1982 by Faber, *The Rattle Bag* contained several translations by Heaney, one of which was "The Names of the Hare." Heaney had first published the translation from Middle English in the *Poetry Ireland Review* in the Spring of 1981, and it was later collected with revisions in *Opened Ground* (1998). The poet had apparently been drawn to "The Names of the Hare" while gathering material for *The Rattle Bag*. The broadside edition of *The Names of the Hare* appeared in 1992 and was published by the Waddington Galleries, Ltd, London, in an edition of 250 copies signed by Seamus Heaney and Barry Flanagan.

The broadside carries the titles *Les nouns de vn en leure engleis* and *The Names of the Hare* over two columns, respectively, above which are three golden hares by Flanagan. On a blue background, the poems are printed in black, with gold versals two lines deep. Flanagan, a Welsh sculptor, had begun to receive attention in the late 1970s for his works depicting a variety of animals, of which the bronze hare was one of the most highly regarded. The anthropomorphic hares frolicking in the air on the broadside above the poem capture the creatures' playfulness and complement the playfulness of the poem itself. Heaney says of the broadside: "And when I saw Barry Flanagan's hares leaping in gold through the Marian blue of that poster poem, I rejoiced in the sheer gleefulness and allusiveness of it, since the poem is essentially a litany, an invocation of the names of the hare in a repetitive, votive cadence reminiscent of the Litany of the Virgin. The domed shape of the panel and the gilt treatment make the leapers look like putti." From a more secular perspective, *The Names of the Hare* is a list of imaginative sobriquets, which begins:

> *The hare, call him scotart, / big-fellow, bouchart,*
> *the O'Hare, the jumper, / the rascal, the racer.*
> *Beat-the-pad, white-face, / Funk-the-ditch, shit-ass.*

With its large blue domed panel, the broadside is one of Heaney's most attractive. There is no record of how the collaboration between poet and sculptor was initiated, but it was obviously mutually beneficial, and Heaney certainly enjoyed the results. "The Names of the Hare" poem was reprinted in an exhibition catalogue *The Names of the Hare: Large Bronzes by Barry Flanagan, 1983–1990*, Yorkshire Sculpture Park, June–August 1992.

The Names of the Hare / Les Nouns de un leure en engleis, Waddington Galleries, Ltd., 1982.
printed at Hillingdon Press, broadside 250 numbered copies
signed by author and artist, 43.5 × 56 cm.

S EAMUS HEANEY'S RELATIONSHIP with Harvard University began in the spring semester 1979 at which time he served as a visiting lecturer. Heaney had met the famous Harvard literary critic Helen Vendler a few years before in Sligo, Ireland, at the Yeats International Summer School. Their friendship and professional relationship would grow over the years and was paralleled by the strengthening of Heaney's connection to the university and local communities of the Cambridge area. Several limited publications, such as *Mint* and *Poet's Chair*, are the direct result of these friendships and professional ties.

Mint, published in 1991, is "dedicated to the Corbett family of Boston, in whose home the author has enjoyed many a meal of minty soup and lamb." *Poet's Chair*, published in 1993, "was produced for distribution at a gala" honoring "Robert and Jana Kiely in their twentieth year of service as Master and Associate Master of Adams House, Harvard University." Heaney's accommodations while in residence were located in Adams House. The poem first appeared as "Here for Good" in the *Times Literary Supplement* in January 1993 and was collected with revisions as "Poet's Chair" in *The Spirit Level*. "Mint" first appeared in *Soho-Four* in 1991 and was also collected with revisions in *The Spirit Level*.

Mint and *Poet's Chair* were published by William B. Ewert of Concord, New Hampshire. Ewert (1943–2001), a recognized authority on Robert Frost, had published limited editions and art books on other poets, including May Sarton, Donald Hall, Galway Kinnell, John Updike, and W. D. Snodgrass. *Mint* was published in an edition of 136 copies signed by the artist and poet. The woodcut is printed in reddish brown on copies numbered 1–100. The woodcut of the 36 copies, numbered 1–36, is hand-colored. The original woodcut was designed by Mary Azarian.

The linoleum block illustration for *Poet's Chair* was by Dimitri Hadzi and resembles Hadzi's illustrations in the limited edition of *Keeping Going*. Ewert published a limited edition of *Poet's Chair* numbered 1–100 and signed by the poet and the artist. This edition was printed by hand on cream colored bond paper at Bow and Arrow Press, Cambridge, Massachusetts. Ewert also published an edition of 1,000 copies of *Poet's Chair* printed in green on flecked tan paper and printed by the office of the Harvard University Publishers.

Mint, William B. Ewert
publisher, Concord,
New Hampshire,
printed at Firefly
Press, Somerville,
Massachusetts,
May 1991, woodcut
by Mary Azarian,
broadside 136 copies
signed by author and
artist, 25.5 × 48 cm.

MINT *by Seamus Heaney*

It looked like a clump of small dusty nettles
Growing wild at the gable of the house
Beyond where we dumped our tins and bottles.
Usual and unverdant, a bit like us.

But, to be fair, it also spelled promise
And newfangledness in the yard of our life,
As if something vivid and tenacious
Sauntered in green alleys and grew rife.

The snip of scissor blades, the light of Sunday
Mornings when the mint was cut and loved:
My last things will be first things slipping from me.
Yet let all things go free that have survived.

Let the smells of mint go heady and defenceless
Like inmates liberated in that yard.
Like the disregarded ones we turned against
Because we'd failed them by our disregard.

Seamus Heaney

WILLIAM B. EWERT, PUBLISHER · CONCORD, NEW HAMPSHIRE
"Mint" is dedicated to the Corbett family of Boston, in whose home the
author has enjoyed many a meal of minty soup and lamb. Text copyright
1991 by Seamus Heaney. Original woodcut copyright 1991 by Mary
Azarian. 136 copies, designed by John Kristensen, were printed at Firefly
Press, Somerville, Massachusetts, in May 1991. This is copy 22/36

Poet's Chair, William B. Ewert publisher, Concord, New Hampshire, printed by Bow and Arrow Press, Cambridge, Massachusetts, 1993, broadside 1,100 copies, 100 signed by the author and the artist, an additional 50 roman numeral copies and indeterminate number of *hors commerce* copies, 25.5 × 47 cm.

Poet's Chair

My father's ploughing one, two, three, four sides
Of the lea ground where I sit all-seeing
At centre field, my back to the thorn tree
They never cut. The horses are all hoof
And burnished flank, I am all foreknowledge.
Of the poem as a ploughshare that turns time
Up and over. Of the chair in leaf
The fairy thorn is entering for the future.
Of being here for good in every sense.

Seamus Heaney

WILLIAM B. EWERT, PUBLISHER · CONCORD, NEW HAMPSHIRE

"Poet's Chair" forms part of a longer sequence of the same title. Text copyright 1993 by Seamus Heaney. Linoleum block illustration copyright 1993 by Dimitri Hadzi. Design by Gino Lee. This broadside was produced for distribution at a gala celebration held on May 15, 1993, to honor Robert and Jana Kiely in the twentieth year of their service as Master and Associate Master of Adams House, Harvard University. Of a total edition of 1100 copies, 1000 were printed by photo-offset at the Office of the University Publisher and 100 were printed by hand at The Bow & Arrow Press, Cambridge, Massachusetts.

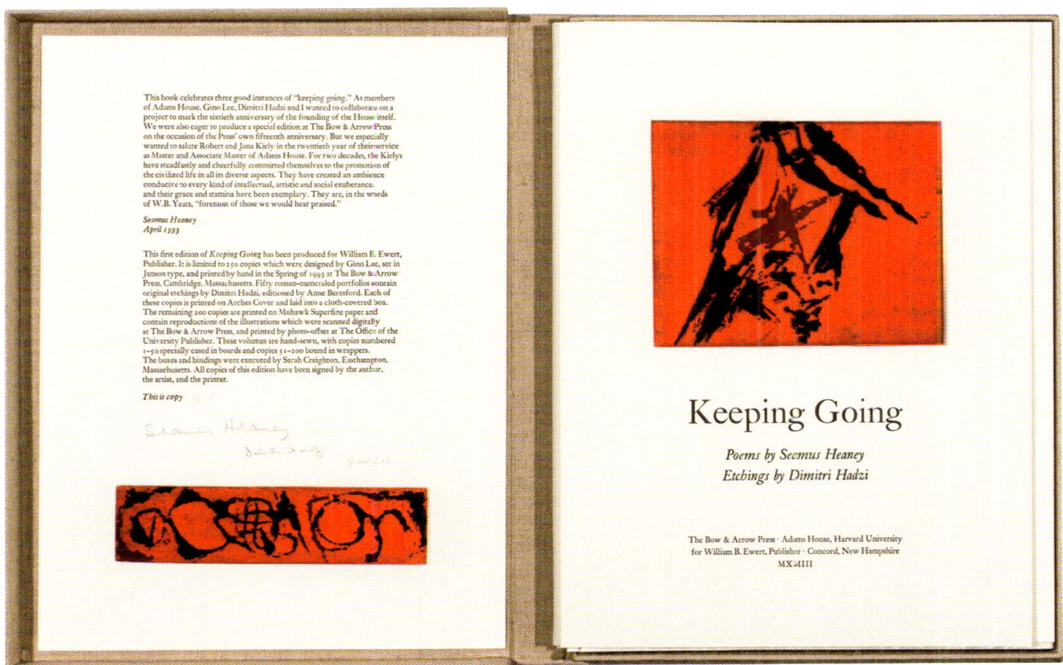

Keeping Going, Bow & Arrow Press, Adams House, spring 1993, produced for William B. Ewert, signed by author, artist, and printer, 250 copies, 50 roman-numbered copies, in portfolio format, contain original etchings by Dimitri Hadzi, 200 numbered and bound copies with reproductions of the illustrations, 22.5 × 30 cm.

17 : *Keeping Going*

WHILE LIVING IN BELFAST in the 1960s, Heaney became friends with several visual artists, many of whom would remain friends throughout his life. One of those early friends was Carolyn Mulholland who was an art student in Belfast when she produced a bronze head of Heaney in 1967 or 1968. Mulholland was primarily known for her portrait heads, but her later works were often commissioned for public spaces. Heaney's poem "Poet's Chair" was a response to one of those public pieces, a bronze chair with sprouting leaves overhead and botanical feet. "Poet's Chair" is one of eight poems collected in the 1993 limited edition *Keeping Going* published by William B. Ewert, designed by Gino Lee, and printed by hand by the Bow & Arrow Press, Adams House, Harvard University, with illustrations by Dimitri Hadzi (1921–2006).

At the time of his death Hadzi was emeritus professor of visual and environmental studies at Harvard, where he had taught sculpture and printmaking for many years. Heaney says of the artist, "In the 1980s, I got to know Dimitri Hadzi in Harvard, and felt at home with him immediately because of his natural *joie de vivre* and his own imaginative at homeness with Greek myths." Hadzi was known for his semi-abstract sculptures in bronze and stone. Like Hadzi, Gino Lee (1962–2011) worked at Harvard where he taught printing-related courses and ran the Bow and Arrow Press located in the Adams House basement. So, in the early 1990s Adams House became Heaney central for more reasons than one.

Keeping Going appeared in three editions: a first edition in boards; a first edition in wrappers; and a first portfolio edition. Published in the spring of 1993 in an edition of 250 copies — 200 numbered copies; 50 roman-numeral unbound copies — with all copies signed by the author, the artist, and the printer. The first portfolio edition numbered I–L contains original etchings by the artist, and the unbound sheets are set in a linen-covered solander box with the title, *Keeping Going*, stamped in gold on a leather label on the spine.

The title poem of the collection, "Keeping Going," is a tribute to the poet's brother Hugh who successfully managed the family farm while dealing with the challenges of petit mal seizures.

> *My dear brother, you have good stamina.* [. . .]

> *I see you at the end of your tether sometimes,*
> *In the milking parlour, holding yourself up*
> *Between two cows until your turn goes past,*
> *Then coming to to the smell of dung again* [. . .]

Seamus Heaney: A Bibliography 1959–2003 does not include information on proof copies because the editors believed that proof copies had become such an ordinary part of the publishing process that listing and describing them was redundant. There is, however, an example of the limitations of our decision — *Apparitions*, the only known copy of which is from the collection of Alan Klein and is included in the exhibition. *Apparitions* appears to be a proof copy of *Keeping Going*. Seamus Heaney would sometimes have two or more working titles for his manuscripts. For instance, *Wintering Out*, Heaney's third volume had the working title *Winter Seeds*, and *Midnight Anvil* was a working title for *District and Circle*, his eleventh volume. However, it is rare for the working title to make it to the proof stage since Heaney usually had things pretty well wrapped up by this point in the publishing process. Of the eight poems in both volumes, three poems in *Apparitions* do not appear in *Keeping Going*: "An Architect," "Weighing In," and "Resolutions." Based upon the differences, *Apparitions* is a "harder" volume than *Keeping Going*.

Bog Poems, The Rainbow
Press, 1975, 150 signed
copies, illustrated by
Barrie Cooke, morocco
leather and marbled
boards with tan linen
slipcase, 20 × 25.5 cm.

18: *Bog Poems*

Published in 1975, the same year as Heaney's most acclaimed work *North*, *Bog Poems* is one of the most highly regarded of the limited editions. Illustrated by Heaney's friend, Barrie Cooke, *Bog Poems* captures the intense psychic and political energy experienced by the poet and people of Northern Ireland during some of the most violent years of "the Troubles." Heaney had met Cooke through Ted Hughes, and Hughes's sister, Olwyn Hughes, published the book at the Rainbow Press, which she managed. The first publication to appear with the Rainbow Press imprint was a collection of previously unpublished poems by Sylvia Plath, *Crystal Gazer*, in 1971. The *Bog Poems* publishing project with the relatively young press was immensely important to Heaney who saw it as a "seal of approval" from Hughes, whom he admired greatly.

Ted Hughes and Barrie Cooke were close fishing partners, and their immersion in the wilds of Ireland infused their mythic consciousness, a consciousness shared by Heaney. In 1969, Heaney had reviewed P. V. Glob's book *Bog People*. The photographs of the bog people from northern Europe in Glob's book spoke deeply and directly to the poet who was searching for a way to get at the complexities of the violence in Northern Ireland. It was as if these bodies, the bodies of prehistoric sacrificial victims, came straight from the collective unconscious and were pre-packaged archetypes. Compressed between the covers of the limited edition, *Bog Poems* is Heaney's most powerful response to the Troubles. Cooke's primitive images concentrate the attention on the prehistoric roots of the conflict as well as illustrated what Heaney called the "bushman" in the "brushman."

Published in an edition of 150 hand-numbered copies signed by the author, *Bog Poems* appears in two covers — one with marbled boards and one with papyrus-covered boards. There are several other differences between the two bindings; however, no priority has been determined for the different bindings. All eight *Bog Poems* were collected in *North*. Heaney associates two additional poems that appeared in *North*, "The Tollund Man" and "Nerthus," with the *Bog Poem* sequence. "The Tollund Man" affirms its status as one of the most significant of the bog poems in that Heaney resurrects him in "The Tollund Man in Springtime" in his 2006 collection *District and Circle*.

19 : *Ugolino*

THE BLACK LEATHER COVERS of *Ugolino* feel as if they came straight from the medieval tanneries of Dante's Florence. This is the black of the *Inferno*, the leather of languishing and lament. The leather also heightens the rawness, the closeness to the world of the beast evoked by Heaney's translation of Dante's *Inferno*, Cantos XXXIII–XXXIV. Heaney says that he selected this passage because he wanted to draw parallels between the desperation of Count Ugolino and the "dirty protests" that were taking place in 1978 in the Maze prison in Northern Ireland where IRA members and others implicated in the Republican violence were being interned.

Ugolino includes two lithographs by the famous Irish painter and printmaker Louis Le Brocquy. Heaney has commented on the ancientness of the artist's "heads" — abstract images that look as if the portraits were chiseled in translucent slate or constructed of stone shards. Le Brocquy had worked with Liam Miller of the

Dolmen Press in 1967 on one of the printmaker's best-known works, a series of lithographs for Thomas Kinsella's translation of *The Táin*. Le Brocquy would go on to draw a portrait of Heaney in 1981, but the poet never sat for the artist and therefore as Heaney notes, he produced an "image" of the poet. Heaney's admiration for Le Brocquy is captured in "Le Brocquy's Táin," a collection of six tankas — Louis Le Brocquy's "Aubusson Tapestries" (2001) — that was published in an exhibition catalogue.

Ugolino was privately published by Andrew Carpenter of University College Dublin in 1979 in an edition of 125 hand-numbered copies of which 30, numbered 96–125, were for sale. According to the publisher, of the 125 copies, 70 were bound in black goat skin and issued in a paper covered slipcase; 25 were bound in black paper covers and issued without a slipcase; and 30 were bound in black textured morocco and issued in a paper-covered slipcase. Blind-stamping the title, *Ugolino*, on the front cover and spine, is like branding the otherness of the name into the book itself. The name is almost onomatopoetic in its suggestion of the sinister and the ugly. *Ugolino* stands out in Heaney's body of works as a powerful totem text. The poem was collected in Heaney's fourth volume *Field Work* and appears as an omen of more Dante to come in *Station Island*.

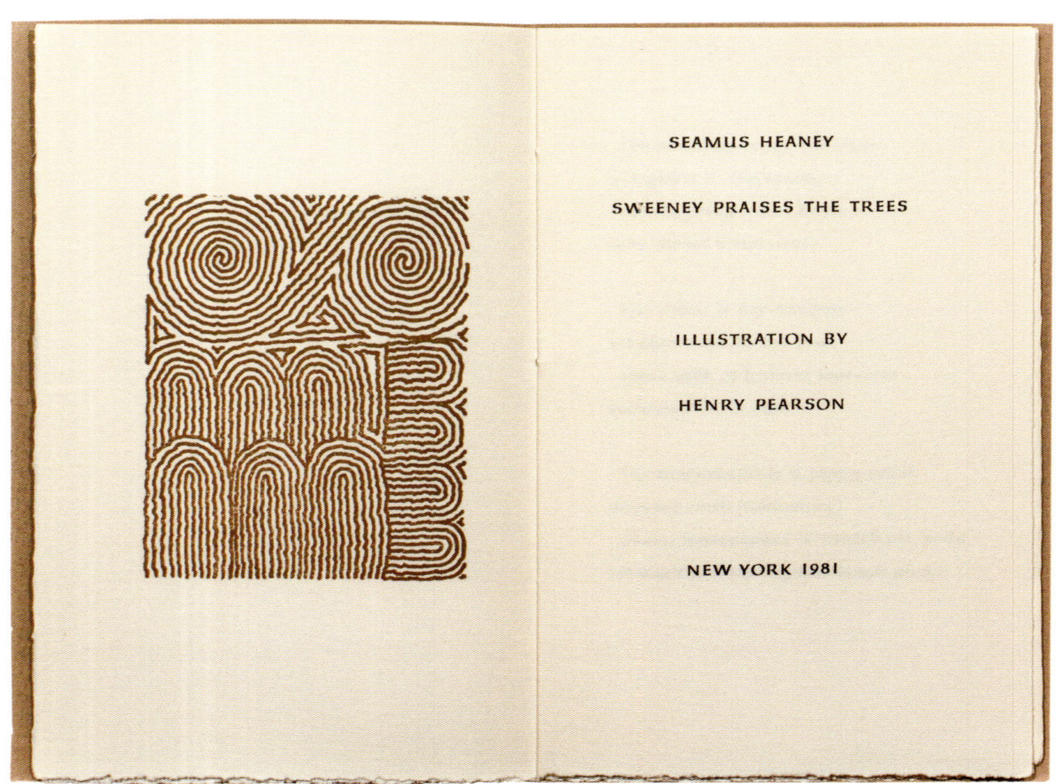

20 : *Sweeney Praises the Trees, Sweeney Astray*

CENTRAL TO THE CELTIC VISION of W. B. Yeats was the Irish mythological warrior Cuchulainn. Capable of grotesque transformations through the power of his "warp spasms," Cuchulainn was the archetypal freedom fighter and one-man-army who defended Ulster in the epic Irish myth *Táin Bó Cuailnge*. He came to symbolize the Irish struggle for independence during the Celtic Revival and the poet as romantic warrior. A more contemporary translation by Irish poet Thomas Kinsella of the *Táin* was published in 1969 by Dolmen Press. Heaney consciously selected a figure from Irish mythology, in contrast to Cuchulainn, that could not be appropriated by the freedom fighters of the Troubles — the mad king Sweeney who was cursed by the Irish Saint Ronan and turned into a bird fated to suffer the woes of an unaccommodated man-creature.

Heaney began translating *Buile Shuibhne* from the Irish in 1972 upon his arrival at Glanmore Cottage. Heaney's version of *Buile Shuibhne* was published by the Field Day Theatre Company in 1983 as *Sweeney Astray*. The Field Day Theatre Company, based in Derry, was founded by Heaney, Brian Friel, and Stephen Rea in 1980, and

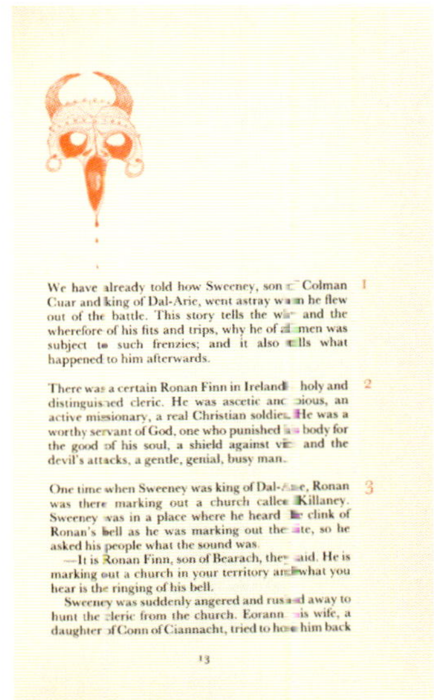

We have already told how Sweeney, son of Colman Cuar and king of Dal-Arie, went astray when he flew out of the battle. This story tells the why and the wherefore of his fits and trips, why he of all men was subject to such frenzies; and it also tells what happened to him afterwards.

There was a certain Ronan Finn in Ireland, holy and distinguished cleric. He was ascetic and pious, an active missionary, a real Christian soldier. He was a worthy servant of God, one who punished his body for the good of his soul, a shield against vice and the devil's attacks, a gentle, genial, busy man.

One time when Sweeney was king of Dal-Arie, Ronan was there marking out a church called Killaney. Sweeney was in a place where he heard the clink of Ronan's bell as he was marking out the site, so he asked his people what the sound was.
—It is Ronan Finn, son of Bearach, they said. He is marking out a church in your territory and what you hear is the ringing of his bell.
Sweeney was suddenly angered and rushed away to hunt the cleric from the church. Eorann, his wife, a daughter of Conn of Ciannacht, tried to hold him back

13

Sweeney Astray was its first major publication. The first edition in boards of *Sweeney Astray* was published in an edition of 1,000 copies. The first edition in wrappers was published in an edition of 3,000. The front cover image of a prehistoric helmet-mask on both Field Day first editions was drawn by Northern Irish artist Colin Middleton whom Heaney had known since the early 1960s in Belfast. The *Sweeney Astray* Field Day publication had a distinctive Northern Irish presence.

Subsequent American and English editions of *Sweeney Astray* were published in 1984 by FSG and Faber respectively. FSG also published a limited edition of 300 numbered copies signed by the author in 1984 that included eight monotype illustrations by Barrie Cooke. In 1992, Heaney, in collaboration with photographer Rachel Giese Brown, produced a new and revised edition of *Sweeney Astray* published as *Sweeney's Flight* by both Faber and FSG. Brown's stunning and atmospheric photographs capture the strangeness of the Irish landscape as it must have appeared to the mad king Sweeney. The world premiere of the photographs from *Sweeney's Flight* took place at Lenoir-Rhyne University in March of 1992.

Heaney had published one section of *Sweeney Astray* in particular prior to the release of the Field Day edition; this was section 40, verses 3–13, "Sweeney Praises the Trees." These passages describing Sweeney having arrived at Gleann na n-Eachtach where he praises the trees of Ireland first appeared in 1978 in the January/February issue of *Quest*. The same stanzas, in a revised form, were then published in 1981 as *Sweeney Praises the Trees*, a limited edition published

Sweeney Astray, Field Day, November 1983, illustrations by Colin Middleton, gray cloth with green dust jacket, 1,000 copies, 14 × 23 cm.

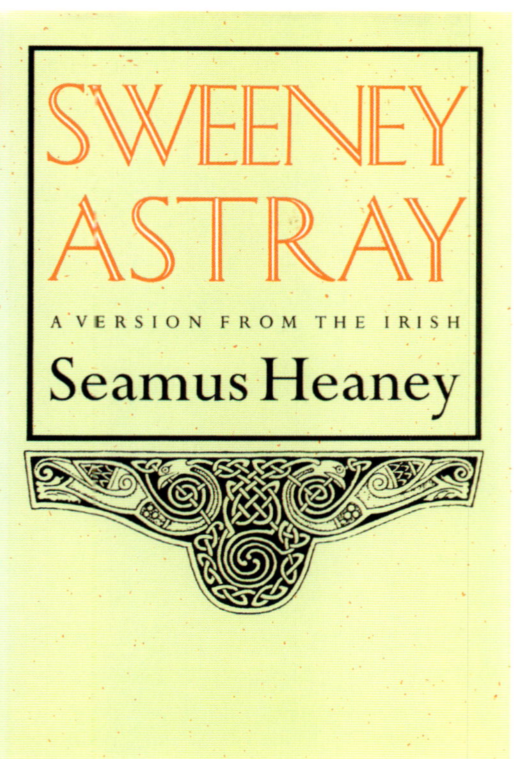

Sweeney Astray, FSG, May 1, 1984, 14.5 × 23.5 cm, published seven months after the Field Day limited edition. The Faber edition was published October 15, 1984.

Sweeney's Flight: Based on the Revised Text of Sweeney Astray, published by both Faber and FSG in 1992, with photographs by Rachel Giese, the only trade edition of a Heaney text accompanied by an extensive collection of photographs.

and illustrated by the American abstract and modernist painter Henry C. Pearson. *Sweeney Praises the Trees* appeared in an edition of 110 hand-numbered copies. Pearson (1914–2006) was a collector as well as illustrator and publisher of Heaney's work. His Heaney projects include several cards of short verses translated from the Irish by Heaney as well as the monumental *Poems and a Memoir* published in 1982 by the Limited Editions Club.

21 : *Poems and a Memoir, The Riverbed, Look Far*

PUBLISHED IN 1982 by the Limited Editions Club, *Poems and a Memoir* is the first significant limited edition of Heaney's work published in America. Essentially a "selected poems" chosen by Henry Pearson, *Poems and a Memoir* includes eight early uncollected poems. Heaney had just published *Poems 1965–1975* (FSG, 1980). *Poems and a Memoir* opens with an introduction by Heaney's friend, the critic and novelist Thomas Flanagan, who is best known for *The Year of the French*, and closes with "The Secret Nests of Derry," an excerpt from the previously published autobiographical essay

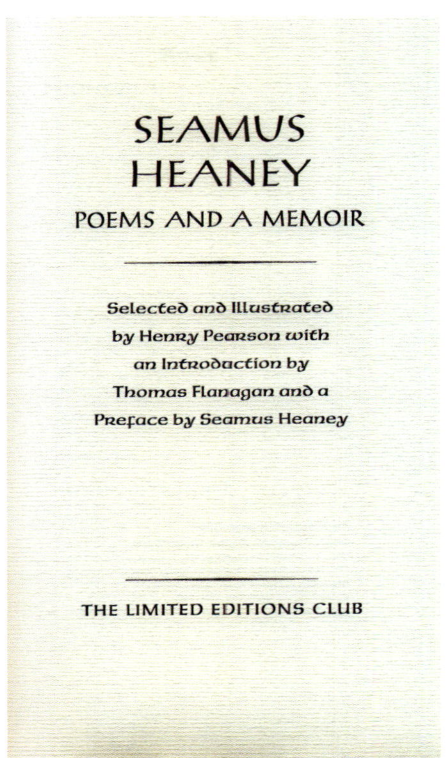

"Mossbawn." When the tome appeared on the shelves and stacks of booksellers, especially at conferences where Heaney was reading, *Poems and a Memoir* (18 × 30.5 cm) eclipsed the surrounding trade editions. Heaney's presence in the U.S. grew exponentially in the early 1980s for a variety of reasons, one of which was the trans-continental schedule of readings that began to fill his calendar.

Published in an edition of 2,000 hand-numbered copies, signed by Seamus Heaney, Thomas Flanagan, and Henry Pearson and issued in a slipcase, *Poems and a Memoir* was a mighty endeavor (6,000 signatures!). In Heaney's preface, one senses the poet's self-consciousness at having his work appear decked out in a Limited Editions Club binding. Reflecting on the place of books — physical books, not books in the abstract — in his life, Heaney writes: "There were books in my life there too, of course, but somehow the world of print was like the world of proper and official behaviour among strangers. You put on your best manners there; when you began to read you were emotionally dressed up and watching your language.... And why, twenty years later, in the privileged forum of a Limited Editions Club preface, am I still harking back to that season of beginnings? Because I am still as surprised and grateful that the liberating, appeasing gift of utterance happened, happened to me!" Heaney's

Poems and a Memoir, Limited Editions Club, The Wild Carrots Letterpress, November 17, 1982, brown leather with brown paper slipcase, 2,000 numbered and signed copies, 18 × 30.5 cm.

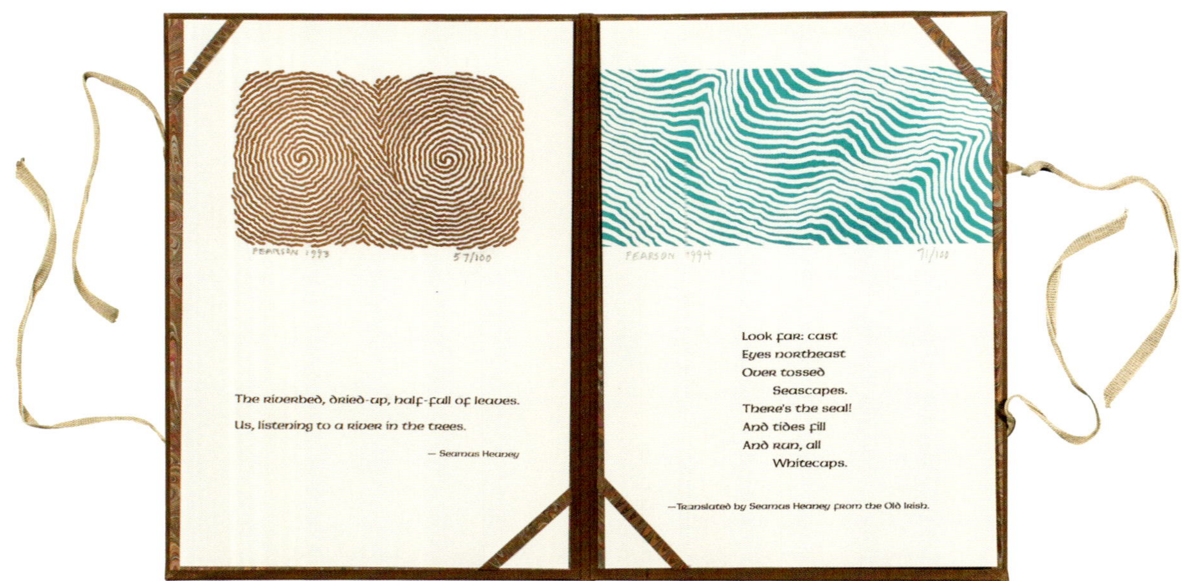

The Riverbed Dried Up / Look Far, poem cards designed and signed by Henry Pearson, 1993, 100 signed copies, 30 artist's proof copies, and 52 out-of-series copies numbered in roman numerals, 18 × 25.5 cm, presentation binding by Carolyn Smith.

strong sense of the mysterious origins of his poetry, origins that predate the poet, are matched by Henry Pearson's relief engravings, which he says were inspired by the stone carvings of Newgrange and other passage graves in the Boyne valley north of Dublin.

The wavering lines in Pearson's engravings possess a dynamism often associated with the prehistoric sense of a world and cosmos in which everything is alive and interconnected. These wavering lines reappear on two more modest Pearson cards — *The riverbed, dried-up, half full of leaves* and *Look far* — published in 1993 and 1994, respectively. "The riverbed, dried-up, half full of leaves" is Heaney's dedicatory poem in *The Haw Lantern*; "Look Far" is his translation from the Irish which first appeared in the Field Day Theatre program for Brian Friel's play *Translations*. The cards, hand-numbered and signed by Pearson, but not Heaney (who was not averse, however, to signing them if asked), seem to be a private project. Both cards were published in limited editions of 100 copies with 30 artist's proof copies and several out-of-series copies.

Henry Pearson (1914–2006) was an early and enthusiastic collector of Heaney. Pearson, who was born in North Carolina and attended the University of North Carolina at Chapel Hill, donated his substantial collection to UNC. Most importantly, Henry Pearson was the first person to compile a checklist of Heaney's works. He published "Seamus Heaney: A Bibliographical Checklist" in *American Book Collector III* in March/April 1982. This was the first attempt to document the variety and ever-increasing number of Seamus Heaney's publications.

22 : Dante's Inferno

S OMEONE WITH A WICKED sense of humor must have selected Seamus Heaney's translation of Dante's *Inferno* for a "Poems on the Underground" poster. One can imagine the sinking hearts of the blurry-eyed racing along underground on the London subway system and looking up only to see, "In the middle of the journey of our life / I found myself astray in a dark wood / where the road had been lost sight of." The poster was part of a "European Poems on the Underground" series and coincided with the publication of *Dante's Inferno: Translations by Twenty Contemporary Poets*, edited by Daniel Halpern. Published by The Ecco Press in 1993 in a limited edition, as well as cloth and paper trade editions, the book contains Heaney's translations of Cantos I–III.

It is amazing how many anthologies place Heaney in the lead-off position when the organizational parameters give them freedom to do so. In the case of The Ecco Press's *Inferno*, it is probably because

Dante's Inferno: Translations by Twenty Contemporary Poets, The Ecco Press, 1993, Cantos I, II, and III translated by Seamus Heaney, with an original etching signed by Francesco Clemente laid in, 145 copies, 125 numbered and signed by all the poets, 20 copies numbered I–XX reserved as the Poets' Edition small folio, quarter black calf and red silk over boards, black silk slipcase, 25.5 × 33 cm.

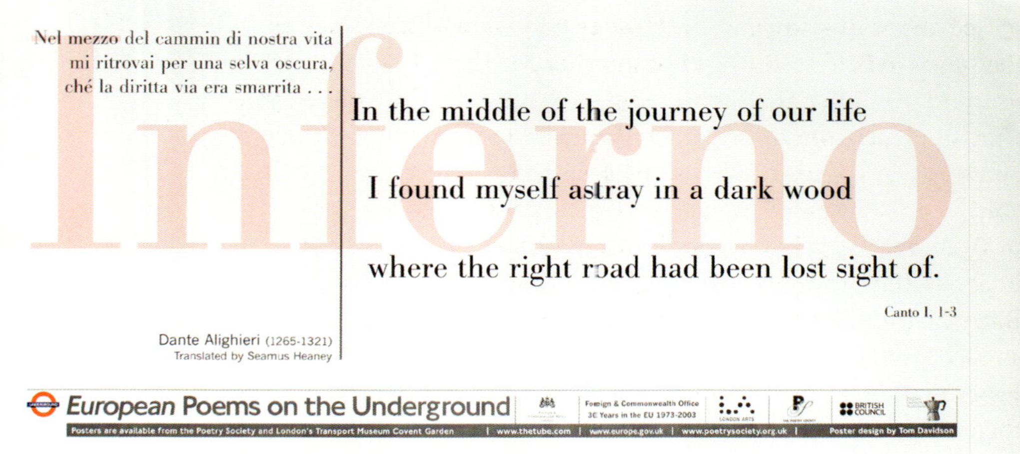

Inferno translated by Seamus Heaney, 2003, London, Poems on the Underground broadside, 60.5 × 28 cm.

Heaney had already translated the first three cantos around the time he was translating the Ugolino section (Cantos XXXII and XXXIII). Heaney had abandoned all hope of translating the entire *Inferno*, even though he really wanted to, because of his limited Italian, which prevented him from achieving the style and tone he desired. Heaney is the only poet to translate three cantos; the other poets translate no more than two.

The limited edition of *Dante's Inferno: Translations by Twenty Contemporary Poets* was published in an edition of 145 copies, 125 of which, numbered 1–125, have been signed by all twenty poets. Each book contains a signed unbound color etching created especially for this edition by Francesco Clemente. Twenty additional copies, numbered I–XX, are reserved as the Poets' Edition. The introduction is by James Merrill and the afterword is by Giuseppe Mazzotta, the Sterling Professor of Humanities for Italian at Yale.

23 : *The Cure at Troy, Burial at Thebes*

ACCORDING TO HEANEY, one of Brian Friel's main objectives when he helped to form the Field Day Theatre Company was to induce poets to write for the stage. Heaney responded to the Irish playwright's directive with his 1990 translation of Sophocles' *Philoctetes*, the full title of which is *The Cure at Troy: A Version of Philoctetes by Sophocles*. Heaney's title was designed to help demystify the play and to reference the Northern Irish desire for a cure for the ongoing violence. The play was published by Field Day in an edition of 500 numbered copies signed by the author. The Field Day first edition includes a list of characters, first production cast and production crew, and a loose erratum slip. The dust jacket has a color reproduction of a painting by Basil Blackshaw of a boat being tossed about in a stormy sea. Heaney had known Blackshaw since the 1960s in Belfast, thus adding another Northern Irish dimension to the book. The first English edition, bound in stiff paper covers with an illustration of two arrows and a bow, was published simultaneously in October of 1990 by Faber in association with Field Day. The first American edition in boards was published by FSG in December 1991; 1,009 copies were printed. This edition has an image of Philoctetes by the eighteenth century Irish painter James Barry on the front cover. The Field Day and FSG dust jackets clearly show the influence of the poet on the design process. However, the Faber marketing department seemed reluctant to move away from their logocentric branding on the cover.

The world premiere of *The Cure at Troy* took place at the Guildhall in Derry, Northern Ireland, on October 1, 1990 — the political significance of the opening venue is obvious. Heaney returned to Sophocles in 2004 with his translation of *Antigone*, which he titled *The Burial at Thebes*. Commissioned to mark the centenary of the Abbey Theatre in Dublin, the play opened on April 5, 2004. Reviewers were divided on whether Heaney's not so oblique references in the play to George W. Bush's post 9/11 policies and actions had compromised the tragedy's universality. Heaney has described a few of Creon's phrases as "Bushisms" and acknowledged the influence that Bush's war on terrorism had on his translation. In sharp contrast to the Faber corporate cover of *The Cure at Troy*, the dust jacket for the first edition of *The Burial at Thebes* published by Faber uses an image by Jan Hendrix from a limited edition of Heaney's work titled *The*

CLOCKWISE FROM TOP:
The Cure at Troy: Field Day, October 1990; Faber, October 1990; FSG, December 1991.

The Burial at Thebes, Faber and FSG editions, whose jackets indicate a translation and a "version," respectively, reflecting the complexities of Heaney's relationship with the original Greek text and the anxieties of the publishers' marketing departments.

Golden Bough (1992). The gold and black abstract image on the cover captures the dark realities mined in the play.

The classical origins of the play are also made manifest in the FSG dust jacket for the first American edition in boards. The cover art by Heaney's friend and Harvard colleague Dimitri Hadzi is titled *Thebes II*. The bronze sculpture looks larger in the cover image than it is (33" × 14½" × 11½"), which gives the three columns a monolithic presence. The three pieces welded together suggest the theme that Heaney highlighted in his translation: the individual conscience caught between the laws of the gods and the laws of the state. Interestingly, the title on the FSG cover and title page reads *The Burial at Thebes: A Version of Sophocles' Antigone*, while the Faber cover and title page read *The Burial at Thebes: Translated by Seamus Heaney*.

Heaney prefers to describe his encounters with works not written in English as "versions." For example, all of the editions of *Sweeney Astray* and *The Cure at Troy* use "a version." For individual poems and shorter works Heaney often will use "after," as in two poems from *Human Chain*: "A Kite for Aibhín, after 'L'Aquilone' by Giovanni Pascoli" or "A Herbal, after Guillevic's 'Herbier de Bretagne.'" "Version" says creative interpretation or adaptation, while "translation" says poetic or linguistic equivalent.

Consequently, in canonical works, like *Beowulf*, which have a long and rich cultural (and academic) presence, Heaney brings with him the authority of the translator. Another difference between the Faber and FSG editions, is that the American "version" of *The Burial at Thebes* includes a note by Heaney following the text of the play. The note explains why his work is *not* a translation by describing the personal, literary, and historical influences that informed Heaney's "version" of *Antigone*. There is essentially a categorical difference in using different English and American titles for the same collection, as in *Selected Poems 1965–1975* and *Poems 1965–1975*, than describing a work as a "version" or "translation." Heaney certainly understood this as well as anyone.

24 : *The Golden Bough, The Light of the Leaves*

SEAMUS HEANEY HAS COMMENTED that some of the artists with whom he has worked were already involved in the world of contemporary Irish poetry or poetry in general before they embarked on a particular collaborative project; others, however, came to his work from afar, as is the case of the Dutch artist Jan Hendrix, who illustrated two amazing limited editions: *The Golden Bough: With Screenprints by Jan Hendrix* (1992) and *The Light of the Leaves: Selected Poems by Seamus Heaney* (1999). Many years before

The Golden Bough,
Imprenta de los
Tropicos in Mexico
D.F. and In de
Bonnefant, Banholt,
Netherlands, May
1992, with screenprints
by Jan Hendrix,
Seamus Heaney's
translation of the
Aeneid, Book vi, lines
98–211, English
printed along with the
Latin, 50 signed and
numbered copies and
3 printed *ad personam*,
black boards, black
paper slipcase
24.5 × 37 cm.

the first of these publications, Hendrix had sent Heaney an unsolic-
ited series of screen prints that were responses to his early landscape
poem "The Peninsula." As with several of the artists with whom he
has collaborated, Heaney appreciated the primordial, archetypal
dimension of Hendrix's work. *The Golden Bough* is a translation of
the *Aeneid*, Book vi, lines 98–211. This selection from the *Aeneid*, first
appears in the periodical *Translations* in 1989 (Heaney's father had
died in 1986) and was collected with revisions in *Seeing Things* (1991).
Book vi describes Aeneas's journey into the underworld to meet
the shade of the father. Heaney has referred to the black and gold
leaf images in *The Golden Bough* as "phantasmagoria," which encap-
sulates both the otherworldly quality of the translated lines and the
spectral shapes on the page.

Printed on Lanaquarelle paper, the text for *The Golden Bough* was
hand-set in Bembo — narrow italic for the English and roman for
the Latin — and printed by Hans van Eijk at the Bonnefant Press of
Banholt. The illustrations, five double-page screenprints on a back-
ground of gold leaf, are by Jan Hendrix and were printed by him at

his studio in Mexico City and published in May 1992 by Imprenta de los Tropicos, in Mexico D.F., and In de Bonnefant, Banholt, the Netherlands, in an edition of 50 copies, numbered 1–50 in the press, with 3 copies printed *ad personam*. All copies are signed by the artist and the author at the colophon. The edition binding was by Hans van der Horst of Eenhoorn Binderij, in Amsterdam, with 8 copies being bound in full leather and 45 in paper boards. Both bindings are blocked with a design based on one of the prints.

Whereas *The Golden Bough* is an occasional work closely connected to the poet's life, the details of which are described in the volume's "Postscript," *The Light of the Leaves* seems to be a much more consciously literary work. Heaney was obviously pleased with the results of the artistic collaboration as well as with the printing and binding because he contributed a translation, "Poet to Blacksmith," to celebrate the first twenty years of the Hans van Eijk's private press. Published in 1997 in an edition of 43 copies, the poem celebrates the scribal arts and the press that had printed *The Golden Bough*. Published in 1999 by Imprenta de los Tropicos in Mexico D.F., *The Light of the Leaves* is a much more involved book than *The Golden Bough* in terms of the poems, printing, screenprints, and binding. The ten poems by Heaney, all uncollected at that time, were trans-

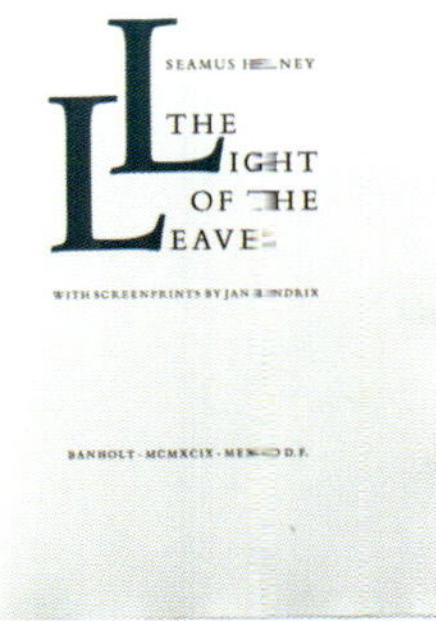

The Light of the Leaves, Banholt, Mexico D.F., 1999, with screenprints by Jan Hendrix, 10 poems in English with translations into Spanish and Dutch, 70 copies printed, 1–63 numbered and 7 copies *ad personam* signed by author and artist, black and white boards, white slipcase, an accompanying portfolio of prints bound in black paper, 24.5 × 36.5 cm.

lated into Spanish and Dutch. The edition consists of 70 copies bound by Philipp Janssen of Binderij Phoenix and numbered 1–63, with 7 copies printed *ad personam*. The screenprint images are printed on very thin Nepalese paper. Each copy is signed by the author and artist. The book is accompanied by a separate set of ten of the prints on a silver background in 7 × 11 cm format signed by the artist and bound in black paper wrappers. Hendrix's images are of abstract landscapes; the sheer paper gives these images a translucence that reflects the title of the book as well as allowing for an imaginative layering or transposition of design. *The Light of the Leaves* is a passing light, a *fin de siècle* twilight, in which many of the poems are haunted by the shades of poets recently deceased. The exquisite beauty of the book heightens the sense of loss, a loss that reminds us ironically of *The Golden Bough*.

25 : *Remembering Malibu*

SEAMUS HEANEY FIRST VISITED the U.S. in 1969 at the invitation of a Virginia literary group. In 1970–1971 he traveled to Berkeley with his family where he was a visiting lecturer. During this time he met the Belfast novelist Brian Moore (1921–1999) who had moved to Malibu, California, in 1964. Heaney re-

Remembering Malibu
by Seamus Heaney

for Brian Moore

The Pacific at your door was wilder and colder
than my notions of the Pacific

and that was perfect, for I would have rotted
beside the luke-warm ocean I imagined.

Yet no way was its cold ascetic
as our monk-fished, snowed-into Atlantic;

no beehive hut for you
on the abstract sands of Malibu—

it was early Mondrian and his dunes
misting towards the ideal forms

though the wind and sea neighed loud
as wind and sea-noise amplified.

I was there in the flesh
where I imagined I might be

and underwent the bluster of the day:
but why would it not come home to me?

Atlantic storms have flensed the cells
on Skellig Michael, the steps cut in the rock

I never climbed
between the graveyard and the boatslip

are welted solid to our insteps.
But to rear and bolt and cast that shoe!

Beside that other western sea
far from the Skelligs and far, far

from the suck of puddled, wintry ground
our footsteps filled with blowing sand.

Printed in an edition of 200 copies at the
Scripps College Press Claremont California 1982

Seamus Heaney

Linoleum block by Carol Wehrmann
Typography by Eileen Walsh

Remembering Malibu,
second edition,
Scripps College
Press, Claremont,
California, 1983,
linoleum block by
Carol Wehrmann,
180 copies, top
and right edges
untrimmed,
46.5 × 32.5 cm.

called his first visit to Moore's home in his memorial comments that appeared in *The Harp*: "Anyhow, it was a revelation to be with the Moores; open house and hospitality, at the personal level; an intimation, at the writerly level, of withdrawal and discipline. The windy shore of the Pacific was as monastic a setting for this late twentieth century artist as the beehive huts had been for monks on the Skelligs a millennium before. From his scriptorium on the edge of a western sea Brian's novels continued...." Heaney remained close friends with the novelist and dedicated the poem "Remembering Malibu" to Brian Moore; the poem was first published in *Fiction Magazine* in 1982 and collected with revisions in *Station Island* (1984).

In 1982, Scripps College Press published the first edition of "Remembering Malibu" as a broadside in an edition of 200 copies with the dedication to Moore. The linoleum block was by Carol Wehrmann, and the typography was by Eileen Walsh. It is reported that as many as 160 copies of this edition of *Remembering Malibu* were destroyed because of dissatisfaction with the appearance of the mixture of text and illustration. It is not clear who was dissatisfied with the broadside, but it is clear that the poem is very difficult to read. The publication information appears on the front of the first edition. A second edition of the broadside was published in 1983 with a different linoleum print by Wehrmann and a design

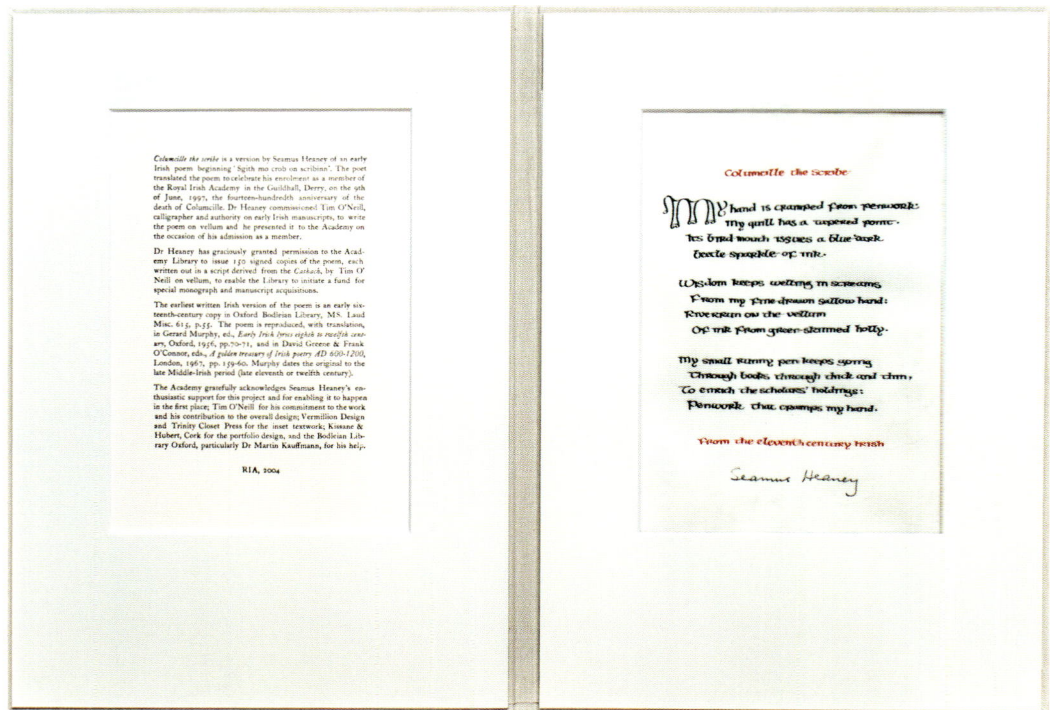

which foregrounded the type. There were 180 copies of the second edition of *Remembering Malibu* printed at the Scripps College Press with the limitation noted as, "This is copy [number written in pencil]." The publication information appears on the reverse of the second edition of the broadside. Scripps College is approximately seventy miles from Malibu, California.

Columcille the Scribe, published by the poet in support of the Royal Irish Academy, 150 copies on vellum with beige linen portfolio, calligraphed and signed by Tim O'Neill and signed by Seamus Heaney, 25.7 × 36 cm.

26 : *Colmcille the Scribe, Alphabets, Hockney's Alphabet*

ON NOVEMBER 30, 2012, President Obama visited Ireland, where one of the most talked about gifts he received was a scroll by Timothy O'Neill, the foremost calligrapher in Ireland of the traditional monastic style. O'Neill had another famous admirer of his art, Seamus Heaney, who worked with the calligrapher on "Colmcille the Scribe," a translation from the eleventh century Irish "Sgith mo crob on scríbbin." On June 9, 1997, Heaney was inducted into the Royal Irish Academy at the Guildhall, Derry. For this occasion, Heaney commissioned O'Neill to produce on vellum "Colmcille the Scribe" in the style of St. Colmcille from the Cathach marking the fourteen hundredth anniversary of his death. The poet gave this to the RIA in appreciation of their legacy and ongoing work.

Colmcille the Scribe,
translated by
Seamus Heaney,
London, Poems on
the Underground,
broadside.

In 2004, the RIA library, with the support of Seamus Heaney, published a limited edition of the poem to help raise funds for the library. Of the 150 copies signed by Heaney, 125 were for sale. "Colmcille the Scribe" was first published in the U.S. in 1999 in the *Gazette of the Grolier Club* (New Series, No. 50). The poem also appeared as part of the "Poems on the Underground" series of posters published by the Poetry Society.

Timothy O'Neill's calligraphy also appears in *Alphabets*, a 2003 broadside publication of section one of the poem "Alphabets" from Heaney's collection *The Haw Lantern*. *Alphabets* was published by the Keough Notre Dame Centre, Dublin, in an edition of 15 copies. The meta-scribal dimension of a scribe transcribing in calligraphy a poem about scribes and calligraphy in "Colmcille the Scribe" finds a contemporary counterpart in *Alphabets*. The poet-as-scribe is one of Heaney's most dynamic metaphors for the creative writing process. This metaphor emphasizes the idea that the poet is as much a conduit through which the poems flow as the source of those poems. The inspired poet may feel as if the poem, line, or word that he has been "given" is more the result of transcription than inscription.

The scribal Heaney often morphed into the printer Heaney, as in the young poet printing out his first letters and using individual letters in poems as typographical and material objects. One of the most famous examples of this use of type is in the closing lines of "Clearances V" from *The Haw Lantern*. The poem uses the memory of the mother and son folding sheets as a metaphor for their relationship: "In moves where I was X and she was O / Inscribed in sheets she'd sewn from ripped-out flour sacks." Because of this typographical predisposition, Heaney was the perfect poet to contribute

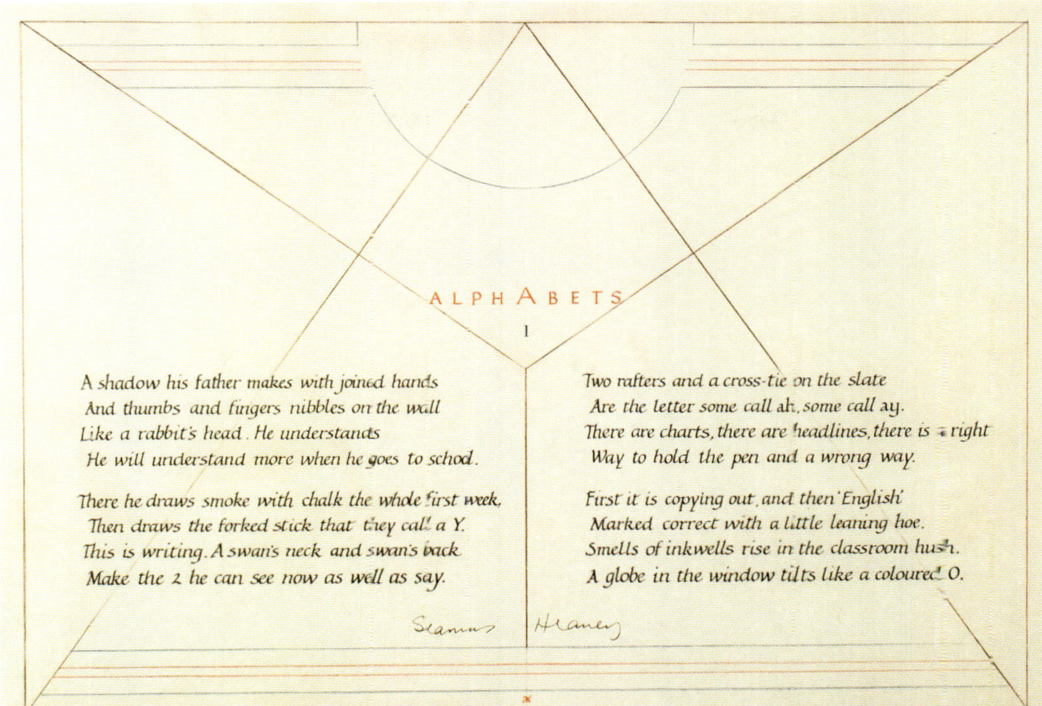

Alphabets, Keough Notre Dame Centre, Dublin, 2003, part one of "Alphabets" from *The Haw Lantern*, calligraphy by Timothy O'Neill, 15 copies, 42 × 30 cm. O'Neill's design responds to the astrological elements of the poem.

Hockney's Alphabet, Faber, 1991, for the AIDS Crisis Trust, drawings by David Hockney and written contributions edited by Stephen Spender, comprising 300 copies printed on Exhibition Fine Art Cartridge paper, specially bound in quarter vellum with handmade Fabriano Roma paper sides, signed by David Hockney, Stephen Spencer, and contributors, 250 numbered copies for sale, a further 26 copies lettered A–Z for the writers. In addition there are 24 copies numbered I–XXIV for William A. McCarty-Cooper, 25 × 33 cm.

"G as in Gaelic," Heaney's contribution to *Hockney's Alphabet*, Faber, 1991, for the AIDS Crisis Trust. The poem is uncollected in a Heaney trade edition.

to *Hockney's Alphabet*. The book was a collaboration between Sir Stephen Spender and David Hockney to raise funds for the AIDS Crisis Trust. Spender solicited the contributions from British and American writers, and David Hockney drew the letters for the Trust. Seamus Heaney was assigned the letter "G" for which he wrote the poem "G as in Gaelic."

Faber published the first trade edition of *Hockney's Alphabet* in 1991. A special edition was published simultaneously, each copy of which was signed by the artist and editor. In addition, Faber published a deluxe edition of 300 numbered copies signed by Spender, Hockney, and twenty-two of the contributors—including Seamus Heaney—250 copies of this edition were for sale. Of the copies not for sale, 26 lettered copies were for the authors and 24 for Spender, Hockney, and the art collector William Marty-Copper (who was HIV positive and died in May 1991). Hockney was unhappy with the quality of the images in the first American edition of *Hockney's Alphabet* published in 1991 by Random House in Association with the American Friends of AIDS Crisis Trust; consequently this edition was withdrawn from distribution. The second American edition was printed in Great Britain in September 1992.

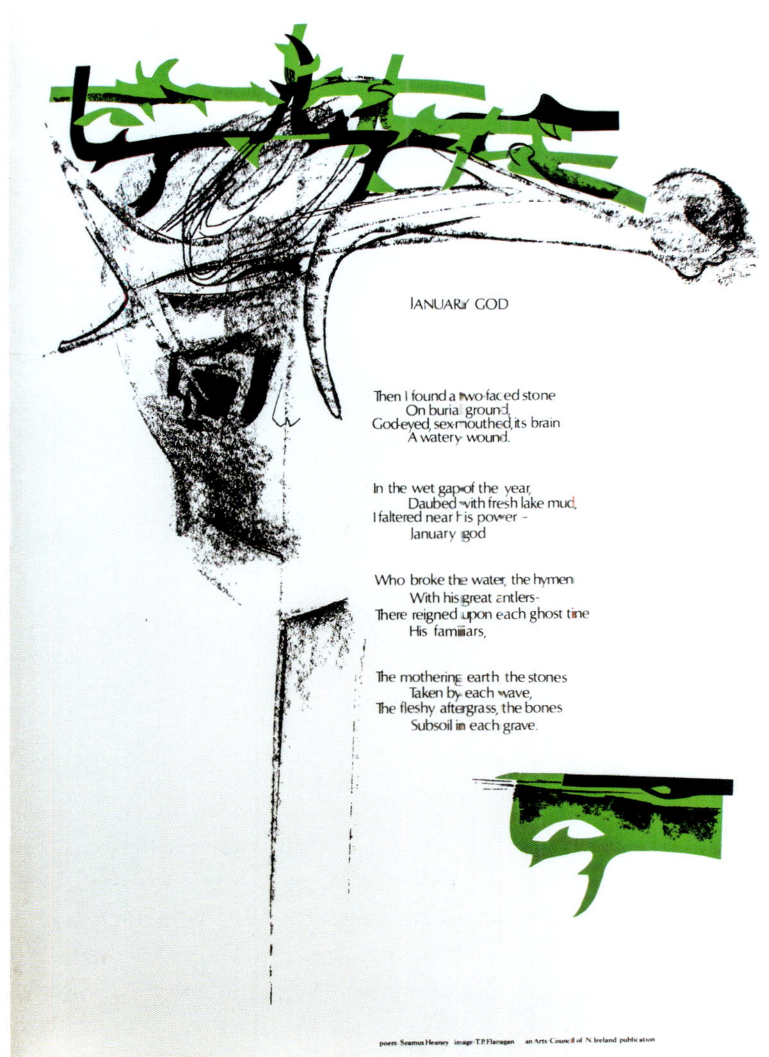

January God,
Arts Council of
Northern Ireland,
1972, broadside,
56 × 76 cm.

27 : *January God*

LIKE THE HUMAN HEAD (preferably severed) that served as a powerful totem and archetypal object among the ancient tribes of Ireland, Seamus Heaney's *January God* has yet to be collected in a Heaney volume. First published in 1972 by the Arts Council of Northern Ireland, the poem appeared as a large broadside with an illustration by the Belfast painter T. P. Flanagan. Heaney has been described as a poet of thresholds; these borders are dynamic points of consciousness between the seen and unseen, the living and the dead, the past and the future. "January God" overlays references to the god Janus with the image of the famous Corleck Head discovered in County Cavan, which many believe was a representation of a fertility god. The Corleck Head is a small stone with three faces carved onto it, each looking a different direction. There is also a suggestion in the poem of the Celtic god Cernunnos, who appears in the form of a deer, thus the antlers in Flanagan's illustration. "January God" is one of those early poems that Heaney did not want to see reattached to the body of his work in a collected form for a variety of reasons. The vast majority of published poems by Heaney are collected; there are around one hundred published but uncollected poems at this time.

From the Republic of Conscience, Amnesty International, Irish Section, December 10, 1985, gray laid covers, 2,000 copies, 14.5 × 21 cm, illustration by John Behan inspired by lines from the poem "From the Republic of Conscience": "Their sacred symbol is a stylized boat. / The sail is an ear, the mast a sloping pen, / the hull a mouth-shape, the keel an open eye."

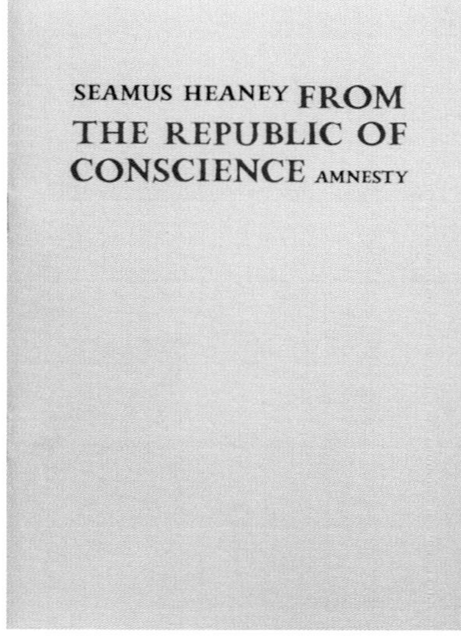

28 : *From the Republic of Conscience*

SEAMUS HEANEY WAS extremely generous when it came to contributing a poem, note, or essay to a cause about which he felt passionate. He has, however, commented on the difficulty of writing a poem in response to requests by specific non-profit publications. One of the most notable cases where he struggled, but finally produced a poem that worked, and worked well, is "From the Republic of Conscience." Published as a pamphlet by Amnesty International in December 1985 in a limited edition of 2,000 copies, "From the Republic of Conscience" was written in response to a request from Amnesty International to commemorate its twenty-fifth anniversary. In his introduction to *From the Republic of Conscience: Stories Inspired by the Universal Declaration of Human Rights*, edited by Roddy Doyle, Heaney gives a detailed account of the request, from the local Sandymount branch of Amnesty International, and his initial inability "to invent 'a verbal contraption' that would be anywhere near as strong as the record of injustice and pain" (recorded in the reports that accompanied the request) and the moment the poem came to him when the pressure was off.

From the Republic of Conscience went on to have a life of its own: in 1987, Parts I and II of the poem were printed in a pamphlet issued by University College Galway's Amnesty International group. The poem was also published in 1989 by the Amnesty International Council and presented to each delegate attending the 1989 International Council meeting in Dublin. In 1993 a broadside of the poem printed on stiff white paper was published by White Pine Press, Buffalo, New York. The apotheosis of "From the Republic of Conscience" came when it was selected as the title for Amnesty International's highest award: The Ambassador of Conscience. Václav Havel, a poet and former president of the Czech Republic, was the award's first recipient in 2003.

Beowulf, Folio Society, 2010. translated by Seamus Heaney, illustrated by Becca Thorne, 18.415 × 27.94 cm.

29 : *Beowulf*

IN ITS NOVEMBER 29, 1999, ISSUE, *Forbes* published "Leadership Lessons from Beowulf" in response to Seamus Heaney's best-selling translation of the Anglo-Saxon poem. The article's author, Tom Post, quotes insightfully from the text and closes by commending Heaney's work for not being "overly literal or stilted," echoing the judgments of more scholarly readers. The section from *Beowulf* where Grendel hears the scop (bard) singing the praises of the Christian god also meets the public head-on in the "1,000 Years

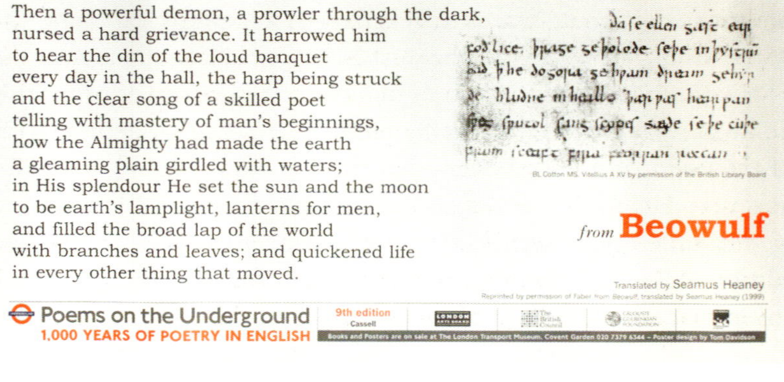

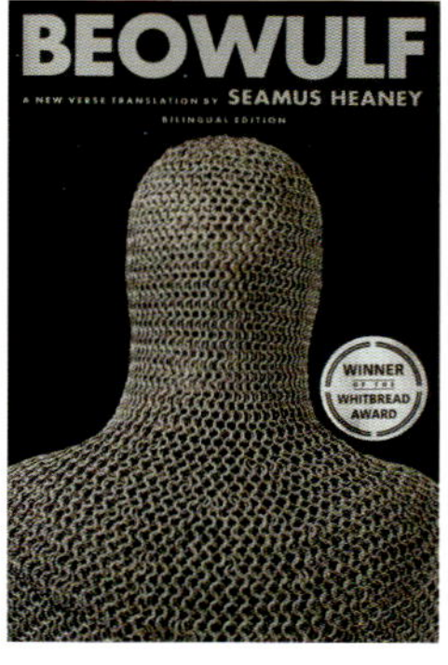

CLOCKWISE: *Beowulf*, FSG, February 15, 2000; *Beowulf*, Faber, October 1999; *From Beowulf*, Poems on the Underground, broadside, ca. 2000.

of Poetry in English" series of "Poems on the Underground." This passage melds together the pagan world out of which Beowulf rises to the Christian world of its author. The Anglo-Saxon sense of doom is lightened by the Christian's belief in a brighter future.

The success of Heaney's translation of *Beowulf* has many sources, but an obvious one is that he has made the poem accessible in a sensible way, as with much of his own poetry. Seamus Heaney was first approached by Norton to translate the poem sometime in 1984 or 1985. The first edition in boards of *Beowulf* was published by Faber in 1999 some fifteen years later. The first lines of *Beowulf* translated by Heaney were published in 1986 under the title "A Ship of Death" with the accompanying information: "'A Ship of Death' is Seamus Heaney's translation of *Beowulf* lines 26–52." Lines 89–98 were published in 1987 as "The Scop" and appeared in *Causley at 70*. Sometime during the early 1990s, Norton asked Heaney if he could recommend another translator, perhaps someone like Ted Hughes, to meet the publisher's deadline for a new translation of *Beowulf*. This was probably the nudge Heaney needed, and by the mid 1990s more sections of the poem started to appear as preludes to the 1999 first edition published by Faber — presumably since Heaney was a "Faber" poet and Norton agreed to the publishing arrangement. The front cover image of the dust jacket of the Faber first edition is by the Irish painter Barrie Cooke. A detail from Cooke's painting *Then Rain* drives home the Irish roots of the poet and the Hiberno-English, Northern Irish etymological roots at the heart of Heaney's translation.

The Faber limited edition was published in 1999 in an edition of 325 numbered copies signed by the author, 300 copies numbered 1–300 for sale, 25 copies numbered 1–xxv reserved for the author. The limited edition is bound in cream, paper-covered boards, front and back covers blank, and issued in a green paper covered slipcase. The Faber limited edition also includes a color reproduction of the opening page of the *Beowulf* manuscript. FSG published the first American edition in boards in February of 2000. In contrast to the Barrie Cooke cover image, the dust jacket of the cover image of the FSG edition is of a photograph of a chainmail-covered torso. This Tolkienesque medieval image emphasizes the Anglo-Saxon origins of the poem and underscores that the FSG first edition is a bilingual text. Heaney's translation of *Beowulf* was included in the 1999 *Norton Anthology for English Literature*. Norton also published the first edition of *Beowulf* in wrappers in 2001 and used the same chainmail cover image as the FSG publication. In the world of literary acclaim, the book's final battle was not with a dragon, but with a wizard wielding a wand of dragonsheart string: *Beowulf* was awarded the 1999 Whitbread Book of the Year Award, surviving a strong showing by *Harry Potter* and plenty of media madness.

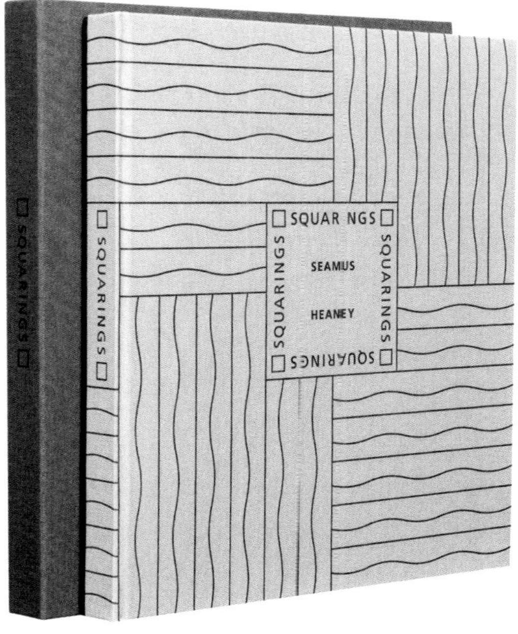

Squarings, The Arion Press, 2003, drawings by Sol Lewitt. gray boards, gray slipcase, 400 numbered copies for sale and 26 lettered copies for complimentary distribution, 26 × 28 cm.

30 : *Squarings, Vitruviana*

I N CELEBRATION OF Seamus Heaney's seventieth birthday, RTE produced a long documentary on the life of the poet, *Into the Marvellous*. The film begins with an animated sequence depicting the scene described in what has become one of Heaney's most referenced poems, "The annals say… ," which is collected in *Seeing Things* as "Squarings, viii." Published in 1991, *Seeing Things* contains the sequence of forty-eight poems titled "Squarings," which is divided into four sections: "Lightenings," "Settings," "Crossings,"

and "Squarings." The poems are twelve lines long with four tercets each. Heaney has said that the "Squarings" form came to him while he was working on his annotations to the W. B. Yeats selections published in *The Field Day Anthology of Irish Literature*. According to Heaney the twelve-line form gave him freedom and opened a new door of inspiration resulting in his writing the sequence in just sixteen months — from September of 1988 to December of 1989.

"Squarings" is only one of several long sequences of poems in Heaney's work, and the poet had considered publishing some of them, like "Sweeney Redivivus," as separate editions. While Heaney chose to leave the sequence embedded in *Seeing Things*, two limited editions of *Squarings* have been published — one containing a selection of twelve poems and another comprised of the entire sequence. Published by Hieroglyph Editions in Dublin, in 1991 (the same year as *Seeing Things*), the first limited edition of *Squarings*, in 100 numbered copies, was signed by the author and the artist. In the first edition, ordinary copies contain twelve poems from the "Squarings" sequence in *Seeing Things* and four lithographs by the Irish artist Felim Egan. An edition of special copies was also published by Hieroglyph Editions. This edition contained an original lithograph signed in pencil by Felim Egan and a quotation in ink in the author's hand and signed by him.

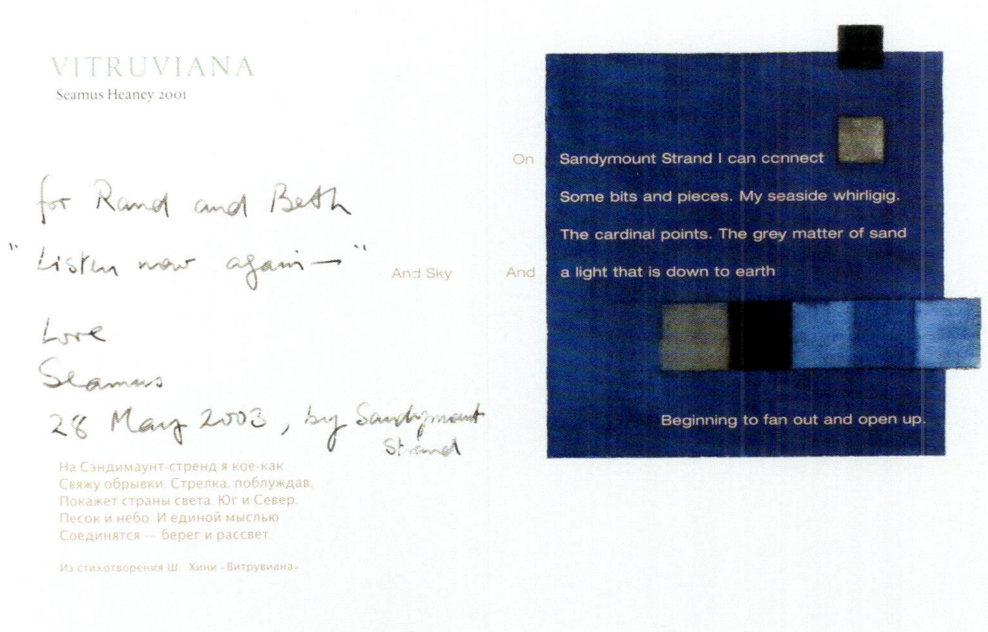

Seamus Heaney and Felim Egan had worked together on a small exhibition in 1986 called "Towards a Collaboration," and Heaney had also contributed to catalogues for Egan's solo exhibitions. The poet was particularly drawn to the airiness and openness of his abstract work, and Heaney acknowledged his appreciation of Egan by dedicating to him a poem, "Vitruviana," which was collected in Heaney's *Electric Light* (2001). The third section of the poem, five lines, provides the text for a folded card also published by Hieroglyph Editions in 2003. The poem is printed over a watercolor by Egan and was published in an edition of 1,000 copies, 1–100 numbered and signed by the artist and poet. An additional 500 cards were published with the poem translated into Russian. These cards were distributed in St. Petersburg where Heaney and Egan participated in the three hundredth anniversary of that city's founding. The five printed lines describe the poet's sense of a corresponding order between man and nature, the ephemeral and the timeless, and thereby reflect the basic organizing principles at work in *Squarings*.

In 2003, Andrew Hoyem of the Arion Press, in San Francisco, published an edition containing all forty-eight "Squarings," poems with forty-eight drawings by Sol Lewitt and an introduction by Helen Vendler. It is unclear how involved Seamus Heaney was in this publication, but Lewitt's drawings bring to the poems a clarity

Vitruviana, Hieroglyph Editions, May 2000, with Heaney's poem "Vitruviana" translated into Russian to be distributed in St. Petersburg, illustration by Felim Egan, card 500 copies 15 × 20 cm folded. Heaney signed this card at Egan's studio near Sandymount Strand.

of concept and vision. Lewitt, who is considered to be the founder of minimal and conceptual art, imagined a way through his drawings to lighten and expand what could have been a heavy block of forty-eight poems. Of all of Heaney's sequences, "Squarings" seems to invite a geometrical treatment of the work both in the art and in the bindings. The twelve-line poem constructed of four three-line stanzas is the poet's dominant form in much of his later poetry. The structure and unity of the twelve lines gave the poet access to a world of light and wonder to balance and perhaps even redress all that oppresses and obscures.

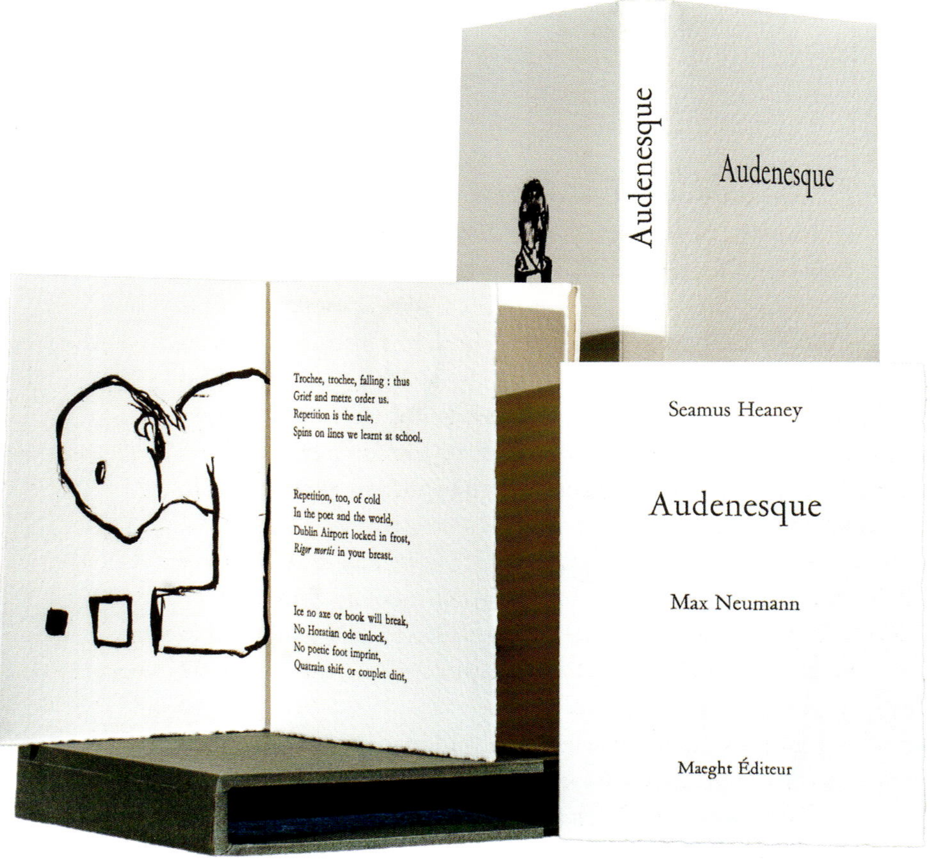

Audenesque, in memory of Joseph Brodsky, Adrien Maeght, May 25, 1998, 100 copies signed by Heaney and illustrator, Max Neumann, original lithographs, loose-leaf pages, green slipcase, 7.5 × 10 cm.

31 : *Audenesque, The Door Stands Open*

SEAMUS HEANEY WAS one of the great elegists of his age. He had the ability to find the necessary words in times of grief and sadness that steadied and centered the self. Whether writing through and out of the deaths of his parents, relatives, friends, community members (known or not), or familiar public figures, most often poets, Heaney's poems always brought with them a for-

tifying but sensitive stoicism. Given his place in history, growing up in Northern Ireland during the Troubles, and his place in the world, friend to many and fearless ally to truth tellers and truth seekers, Heaney's elegies are among his most highly regarded poems. Of his elegies written for poets and artists with whom he had deep relationships, "Audenesque" in memory of Joseph Brodsky (1940–1996) and "Out of This World" in memory of Czeslaw Milosz (1911–2004) are among the last and best Heaney has written. The former poem was collected in *Electric Light* (2001) and the latter poem was collected in *District and Circle* (2006).

Limited editions of these two poems, *Audenesque* and *The Door Stands Open* (which contains Section 3, "Saw Music," from "Out of This World"), are among the most finely designed and produced in the entirety of Heaney's limited publications. The editions share not only powerful poems, "Audenesque" and "Saw Music," but also unique bindings. *Audenesque* is printed in black and red on four loose bifolia of vélin d'Arches paper and placed inside cream handmade covers. *The Door Stands Open* was published in two limited editions, the deluxe edition bound in stainless steel covers wrapped in mixed-media wrapping prepared from a silkscreen collage of articles from the Polish press following the death of Czeslaw Milosz. The book is encased in a slipcase of thick clear Polish glass with a metal alloy spine which reproduces Seamus Heaney's signature in relief and which holds the book between two glass rods.

Both *Audenesque* and *The Door Stands Open* are distinctive limited editions in that they invite a physical engagement with material once one overcomes the preciousness of the objects. Disassembling the contents of both works makes manifest the many dimensions of the

The Door Stands Open, published by the Irish Writer's Centre, Dublin, 2005, printed by the Book Art Museum in Lodz, Poland, on original handwoven and Zanders Zeta paper, bound in stainless steel covers printed in black and folded inside a mixed-media silkscreen wrap, within a frame of twin glass-rods attached to a full mixed-metal spine with the author's signature in relief, in a slipcase of hand-blown clear glass, deluxe edition 50 copies signed by Heaney with a holograph from his poem "Saw Music," 8vo, 18.5 × 30.5 cm.

Audenesque, Adrien Maeght, May 25, 1998.

OPPOSITE: *The Door Stands Open*, published by the Irish Writer's Centre, Dublin, 2005, 8vo, 18.5 × 30.5 cm.

poet's existence and the poems' potential. Waiting inside the slipcase of *Audenesque*, in addition to the finely printed poem, are original lithographs by the German artist Max Neumann. The publisher, Adrien Maeght, is an editor and the owner of the famous Galerie Maeght in Paris. Heaney more than likely crossed paths with him in 1996 while attending the arts and culture festival L'Imaginaire Irelandais in Paris, which explains the French/EU connection. *Audenesque*, the size of a pack of cards, requires special treatment on the shelf and in the hand. It is as if the book embodies the process of poetic distillation and compression. Newman's sparse black and white images of the underworldly archetypal dead also suggest an artistic alchemy, an elemental reduction. The title "Audenesque" is an allusion to Joseph Brodsky's death on January 28, the same date as W. B. Yeats for whom Auden wrote "In Memory of W. B. Yeats." The last stanza of Heaney's elegy refers to *Gilgamesh* and the "house of dust" where all of the dead end up. This allusion explains the brushed ink "Gilgamesh" and red image of a head that appears following the poem in the book. It is as if the page has been quickly stamped like a passport to another, older world.

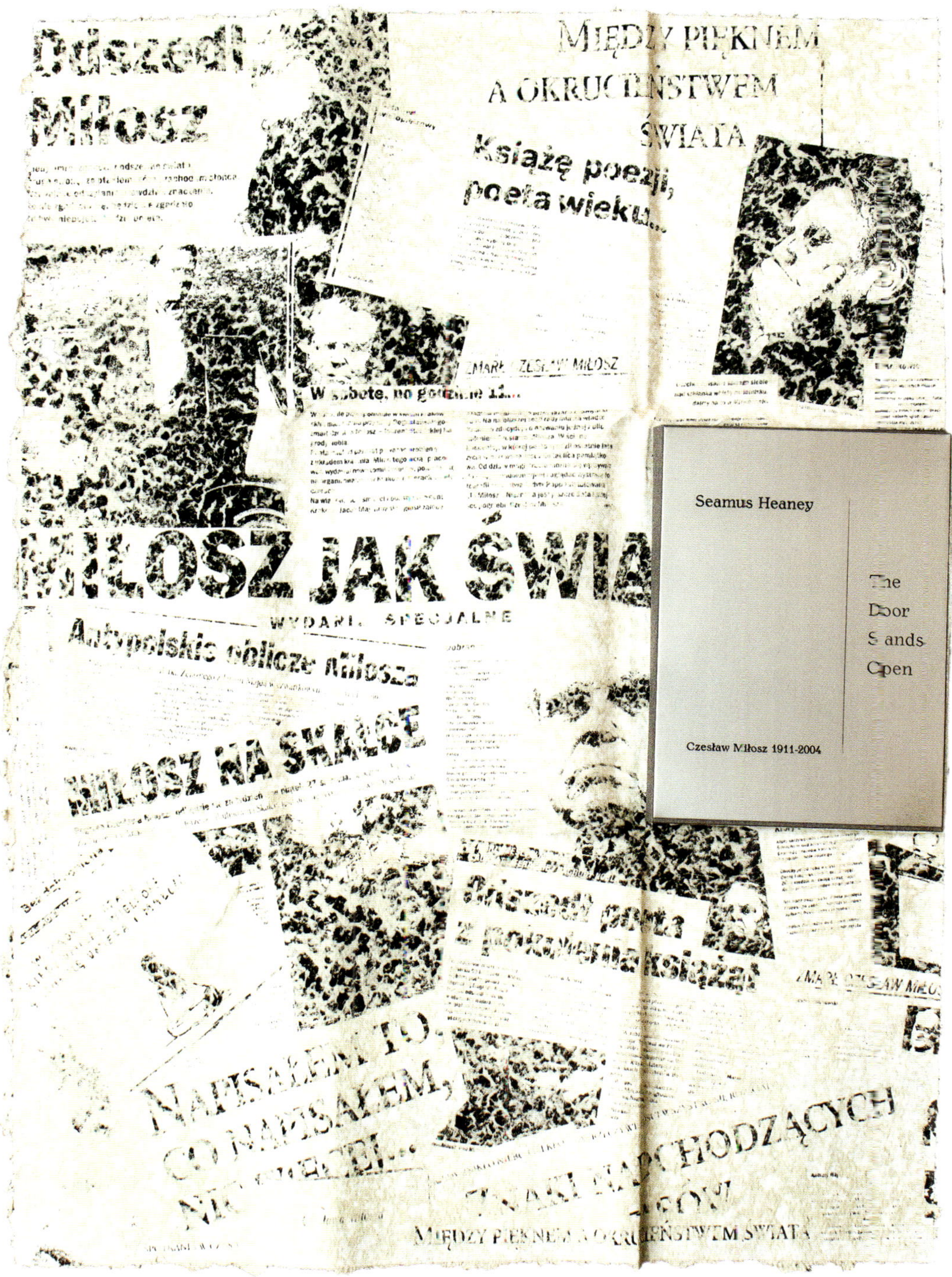

In dramatic contrast to the intimate housing of *Audenesque*, the metal and glass slipcase of the deluxe edition of *The Door Stands Open* is much more formal. While both poets wrote and suffered under oppressive political regimes, *The Door Stands Open* emphasizes the extremely hard political conditions under which Milosz wrote as well as highlighting his Polish heritage. Housed in the book is Heaney's adaptation of Sophocles' *Oedipus at Colonus* (lines 1586–1666), "The Door Stands Open: Czeslaw Milosz," and "Saw Music." In addition, a facsimile of the author's handwritten clear copy of the latter poem is also reproduced. Finally, to underscore Milosz's status as the national poet of Poland, the book contains a prepared mixed-media wrap featuring a silkscreen collage of articles published in Polish newspapers in the days following Milosz's death.

While *The Door Stands Open* was printed by the Book Museum in Lodz, Poland, it was published by the Irish Writer's Center in Dublin. There are many factors that could have played into the decision to make such an elaborately constructed and extremely fragile book, one of which must have been that the Irish Writer's Center wanted to distinguish its publication from the many limited editions of Heaney's poems already in circulation. Another, even more practical reason, could be that since *The Door Stands Open* was published to help raise funds for the Center, the production value must justify the price. Seamus Heaney was keenly aware of the world of collectors (buyers and sellers) that his love of fine books had generated and had become more and more resistant to any limited publication that would seem ostentatious or give the sense of an excessive self-regard. Consequently, *The Door Stands Open* is a show of support for the Center's mission as well as a testament to his admiration for Czeslaw Milosz.

32 : *The Singer's House, The Forge*

O CCASIONALLY, POEMS by Heaney would appear as first separate editions years after first being published and even after being collected in Heaney volumes. Two examples of this were published in 1995: *The Singer's House* and *The Forge*. *The Singer's House* was published as a broadside in 1995, but first appeared in 1977. *The Forge* was published as a broadside in 1995 as well, but first appeared in 1966. The former broadside was commissioned and published by the poem's dedicatee, David Hammond, and the latter appeared as a result of the artist's, Breon O'Casey's, enthusiasm, as well. Heaney obviously consented to both projects, but perhaps for different reasons and through different channels.

Seamus Heaney had known David Hammond in Belfast in the 1960s before the Troubles began. Hammond was very much a part of the cultural scene in Northern Ireland. He was a musician, broadcaster, and filmmaker who worked with Heaney on many projects, including the May 1968 "Room to Rhyme" tour and as a director

of Field Day Theatre Company. Heaney referred to Hammond as a free-spirit whose pluralism represented a way forward through the sectarianism of Northern Ireland. During the Troubles, Heaney and his family spent time during the summers in the west of Donegal where Hammond had a house. In retrospect, Heaney saw the time he spent in the west with Hammond and other Northern Irish writers as a form of protest and not escape.

The broadside, *The Singer's House*, published in 1995, captures this sense of invigorating freedom and rejuvenating friendship in the airiness and light of the watercolor image. The poem "The Singer's House" was first published in *Thames Poetry* in November 1977 and collected with revisions in *Field Work* (1979). The broadside was commissioned and published by David Hammond and features a color screenprint by James Allen. Allen was born in County Armagh and studied at the Belfast College of Art, 1961–1965. He was the director of the Belfast Print Workshop, 1980–2002, when commissioned by Hammond to create a screenprint for *The Singer's House*. The broadside image of the house seems to rest on the solid foundation of the

The Singer's House, David Hammond, 1995, printed by Belfast Print Workshop, screenprint by James Allen, mouldmade paper, manuscript facsimile below, broadside 30 copies and 6 artist's proofs of which this is the sixth, 94 × 76 cm.

THE FORGE

The Forge by Seamus Heaney

Etching by Breon O'Casey

ALL I know is a door into the dark.
Outside, old axles and iron hoops rusting;
Inside, the hammered anvil's short-pitched ring,
The unpredictable fantail of sparks
Or hiss when a new shoe toughens in water.
The anvil must be somewhere in the centre,
Horned as a unicorn, at one end square,
Set there immoveable: an altar
Where he expends himself in shape and music.
Sometimes, leather-aproned, hairs in his nose,
He leans out on the jamb, recalls a clatter
Of hoofs where traffic is flashing in rows;
Then grunts and goes in, with a slam and flick
To beat real iron out, to work the bellows.

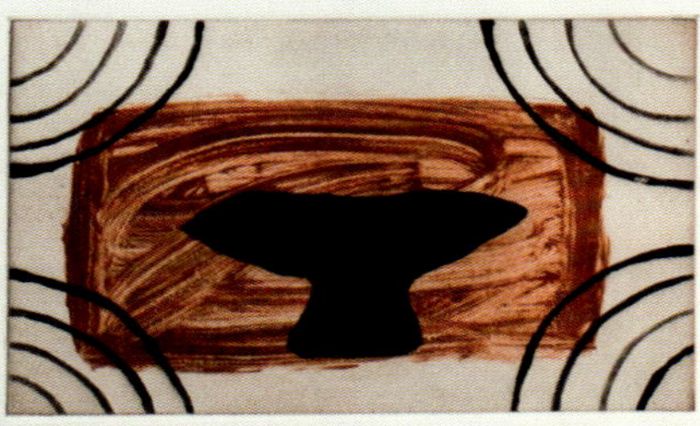

The Forge, broadside with etching by Breon O'Casey, 1995, text printed by Simon King, etching printed by Hugh Stoneman, 50 copies signed and numbered by the artist, plus 5 artist's proofs, untrimmed handmade paper, single leaf folded within a paper portfolio, 38 × 51 cm.

poem printed below it. The spirit of the poem literally supports and even lifts up the house like the poet's celebratory lines which close the poem: "Raise it again, man. We still believe what we hear."

The Forge represents Breon O'Casey's renewed interest in his Irish roots that took place near the end of his career. The son of playwright Sean O'Casey, Breon was born in London, but spent the majority of his life in Cornwall. Hugh Stoneman, the printer of the etching, had just moved to Cornwall in 1995, the year the broadside was produced. While *The Forge* was conceived in O'Casey's studio at Trungle Farmhouse, Mousehole, Cornwall, it seems to have come out of nowhere. Although Heaney was not involved in the project—emphasized by his missing signature, a signature one would expect on a broadside of this size and this late in the poet's career—the project makes sense in the context of O'Casey's body of work.

One of the artist's dominant shapes is that of the anvil, so "The Forge" would seem like a natural choice. The Celtic spiral printed on the cover serves as a visual link between the poem and O'Casey's etching and adds an Irish aspect. O'Casey's symmetrically shaped anvil is not Heaney's forge that is "Horned as a unicorn, at one end square." There is no attempt to be literal; the artistic impulse seems to be driven by the mystical potential of the image. This "door into the dark" is suggested by the four curved lines that seem to be radiating out from sources beyond the four corners of the etching and moving from the foreground towards the pitch black anvil in the center like sound waves, word waves returning from beyond. These are perhaps the magnetic pulses that drew O'Casey to the poem, inspiring one of the most potent responses to a Heaney poem to date.

33 : *Glanmore Sonnets, Hedge School, The Blackbird of Glanmore*

SEAMUS HEANEY HAS OFTEN SAID that his imagination had been shaped for all practical purposes by 1957, the time he left home to attend boarding school in Derry. Of course, his imagination continued to deepen and develop as his world and consciousness grew, but his home place, Mossbawn and the surrounding territories, were always at the center of his poetic being. Throughout his life, and especially after being awarded the Nobel Prize — the earthquake experience of which would disorient and decenter even the most grounded of poets — Heaney described his sense of the original place as the center from which his life experiences rippled. Since place is so essential to his poetry and life as a poet, Heaney naturally (and luckily and gratefully) found a place in the Irish Republic that would serve as another creative center, Glanmore Cottage. This is the cottage, located about forty minutes south of Dublin in County Wicklow, to which Heaney brought his family in 1972. They rented

Glanmore Sonnets, published by Monika Beck, October 10, 1977, illustrations by Cecil King, signed by Heaney and King, unbound sheets with four poems by Heaney and four abstract oil paintings by King, 50 copies total, 35 in blue cloth-covered portfolio of which 25 were distributed in Ireland and 10 in Germany, the other 15 copies bound in black wrappers and distributed in Germany, 35 × 35 cm.

Hedge School,
Charles Seluzicki,
September 1979,
sonnets selected
from the series
"The Glanmore
Sonnets" in
Field Work, color
woodcuts by Claire
Van Vliet, printed
by Janus Press,
Newark, Vermont,
285 copies signed
by author and artist,
brown card,
18 × 28 cm.

the cottage from Ann Saddlemyer, a Yeats scholar at the University of Toronto, who had edited editions of the work of Lady Gregory and J. M. Synge. Saddlemyer sold Glanmore Cottage to the Heaneys in 1988. The importance of the relationship and these exchanges is acknowledged by the fact that Saddlemyer is the dedicatee of the volume *District and Circle* and "The Glanmore Sonnets" as collected in *Field Work* (1979).

"Exposure" is the final poem of Heaney's fourth volume, *North*. The poem is a reaction on one level to Heaney's growing profile on the Irish and international poetry scene, which was attracting plenty of media attention especially as the Troubles worsened. From the angle of limited editions of his work, the poet perhaps found himself over-exposed, as well, by the time he published *Glanmore Sonnets* (1977) and *Hedge School* (1979). The former publication contains four poems that were collected in *Field Work*, and the latter contains the ten sonnets collected in *Field Work*. As with another limited publication of a sequence of poems, such as *Squarings*, a selection from the sequence appeared before the complete sequence, and the publications were separated by time and geography. *Glanmore Sonnets*, published and printed in Germany, contains four abstract oil paintings by Cecil King (1921–1986) who was born in County Wicklow.

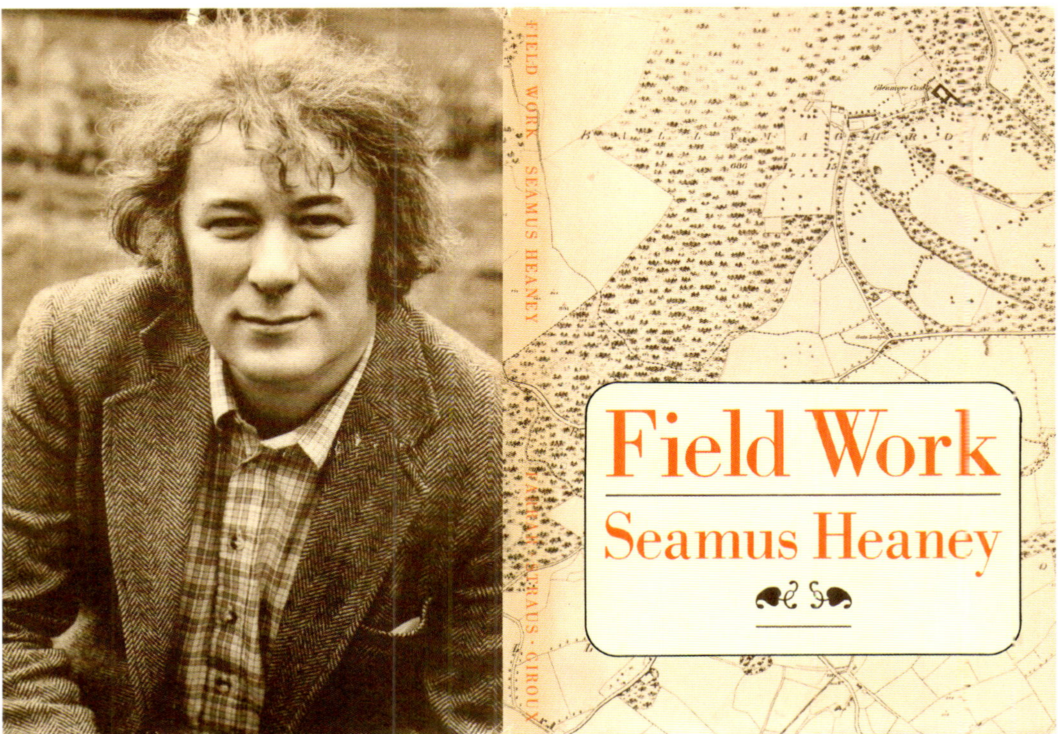

Heaney says that the images by King, best known for his minimalist "hard-edged" paintings, were probably more a response to the four-square shape of the sonnets than to the poems' images.

In contrast to the abstract feel of *Glanmore Sonnets*, the representational color woodcuts by Claire Van Vliet in *Hedge School* reflect the organic innerworkings of the entire sonnet sequence. The title *Hedge School* refers to the practice of establishing impromptu schools, some of which were under or near hedges, in response to the eighteenth century Penal Laws which prohibited Irish Catholics from teaching in an official capacity in public buildings or private homes. Though the courses were highly dependent on the oral traditions, students could also study the classics in the original Greek or Latin. The hedge school is therefore an analogy for the four years (1972–1976) that the Heaney family spent at Glanmore Cottage. *Hedge School* was printed by the Janus Press (which Van Vliet founded in 1955) and is connected to a 1977 limited edition, *Chiasmadon*, by Ted Hughes, published by Charles Seluzicki and printed by the Janus Press. It seems as if Hughes opened the door for this impressive publishing project monumentalizing Heaney's second space, Glanmore Cottage.

Heaney directly links Glanmore, this second space, second center, to his first place and prenatal center in County Derry, in the

Field Work, FSG, 1979.

Field Work, Faber, 1979. The jacket of the Faber edition, published first, incorporates a map of the Glamore Cottage area, as does the FSG first edition, though a different map. In the analog '80s, Heaney's fans used these maps to find the real cottage.

THE BLACKBIRD
OF GLANMORE

On the grass when I arrive,
Filling the stillness with life,
But ready to scare off
At the very first wrong move.
In the ivy when I leave.

It's you, blackbird, I love.

I park, pause, take heed.
Breathe. Just breathe and sit
And lines I once translated
Come back: "I want away
To the house of death, to my father.

Under the low clay roof."

And I think of one gone to him,
A little stillness dancer—
Haunter-son, lost brother—
Cavorting through the yard,
So glad to see me home,

My homesick first term over.

And think of a neighbour's words
Long after the accident:
"Yon bird on the shed roof,
Up on the ridge for weeks—
I said nothing at the time

But I never liked yon bird."

The automatic lock
Clunks shut, the blackbird's panic
Is shortlived, for a second
I've a bird's eye view of myself,
A shadow on raked gravel

In front of my house of life.

Hedge-hop, I am absolute
For you, your ready talkback,
Your each stand-offish comeback,
Your picky, nervy goldbeak—
On the grass when I arrive,

In the ivy when I leave.

— Seamus Heaney

Seamus Heaney
for Rand and Beth, 15 August 2004

An unpublished poem by the Nobel Laureate, printed at The King Library Press
as a keepsake for the 45th W. B. Yeats International Summer School, Sligo
5 August 2004
173/250

The blackbird image, from a wood engraving by Jeffrey Morgan, is the logo of
the Seamus Heaney Centre for Poetry at Queen's University Belfast.

The Blackbird of Glanmore, August 5, 2004, poem by Seamus Heaney printed at
The King Library Press as a keepsake for the forty-fifth W. B. Yeats International Summer School, Sligo,
broadside 250 signed copies, 26.5 × 39 cm. The blackbird image, from a wood engraving by Jeffrey Morgan,
is the logo of the Seamus Heaney Centre for Poetry at Queen's University Belfast.

poem "The Blackbird of Glanmore," first published as a broadside in 2004. The poem, through the power of the poet's imagination and his faith in the ongoing and cyclical power of nature, resurrects in Glanmore (the place) the brother memorialized in "Mid-Term Break," a poem set in his childhood home in Northern Ireland. In addition to connecting the personal past and present of the poem, the blackbird of "The Blackbird of Glanmore" has a literary legacy as noted in Heaney's 2001 translation of "The Blackbird of Belfast Lough" and his poem "Saint Kevin and the Black Bird," collected in *The Spirit Level*. *The Blackbird of Glanmore* features a wood engraving of a blackbird by Jeffrey Morgan, County Antrim, whose works include a portrait of Seamus Heaney. Morgan has strong connections with Queen's University Belfast, and his engraving based upon "The Blackbird of Belfast" is the logo of the Seamus Heaney Centre and the centre's literary publication, *The Yellow Nib*. The blackbird helps to connect the seemingly random dots in Heaney's personal life and publishing life, revealing a dense matrix of organic, integrated relationships and associations.

34 : *I Thought of Walking Round and Round a Space,*
Four Poets for St. Magnus

SEAMUS HEANEY'S WORKING title for *The Haw Lantern* (1987) was *The Stone Verdict*, a title that accurately describes the judicial temperament and public perspective of the majority of the poems. In contrast to the tough stance taken by these poems is a sonnet sequence, "Clearances," written in memory of Heaney's mother Margaret Kathleen Heaney (1911–1984). The sequence occupies an empathetic space in the book and is the open heart of *The Haw Lantern*. "Clearances" is composed of eight sonnets primarily describing episodes from the mother's life and the poet's memories of simple, but poignant times together. *Clearances*, a limited edition of seven of the eight poems, was published in 1986 by the Cornamona Press. In 1986 two "Clearances" poems were published: *[From] Things to Share* and *In Memoriam*. *Things to Share* was the working title for the "Clearances" sequence, and *In Memoriam* was collected as Sonnet 7 in *The Haw Lantern*. *In Memoriam* was printed in a *feuille volante* edition of 20 copies "for the poet's and printer's 'kin and kith'" and was never published. The first separate edition of one of the most famous of the "Clearances" sonnets, Sonnet 8, *I Thought of Walking Round and Round a Space*, was published in 1987 by the Char Press with illustrations by Robert Perkins who also printed the broadside. The monoprint lithograph reproduced the poet's holograph of the poem on a variety of background illustrations.

I thought of walking round and round a space
Utterly empty, utterly a source,
Where the decked chestnut tree had lost its place
In our front hedge above the wallflowers.
The white chips jumped and jumped and skited high.
I heard the hatchet's differentiated
Accurate cut, the crack, the sigh
And collapse of what luxuriated
Through the shocked tips and wreckage of it all.
Deep planted and long gone, my coeval
Chestnut from a jamjar in a hole,
Its heft and hush become a bright nowhere,
A soul ramifying and forever
Silent, beyond silence listened for.

Seamus Heaney / Robert Perlman

Seamus Heaney also published another poem in 1987 titled "In Memoriam" in *Four Poets for St. Magnus*, a project organized by George Mackay Brown. Heaney first met the Scottish poet George Mackay Brown in 1968 when Brown visited Belfast, and the two met again, in 1982, when Heaney traveled to the Orkney Islands. Heaney's poem "Would They Had Stay'd" closes with a stanza dedicated to the memory of Mackay Brown. Brown, a resident of Orkney, helped found the St. Magnus International Festival in 1977. The midsummer festival helped the community maintain an international arts presence, which more than likely made *Four Poets for St. Magnus* possible. It was published on August 20, 1987, on the occasion of the eight hundred and fiftieth anniversary of the founding of the Cathedral of St. Magnus, Orkney. The cathedral also installed a new rose window as part of the anniversary year. The four contributing poets are Seamus Heaney, George Mackay Brown, Ted Hughes, and Christopher Fry. Brown was obviously the organizing force behind *Four Poets for St. Magnus*. The publisher and press disappeared after the celebration publication.

35 : *Testimonies, Höfn*

Testimonies, University of Iowa Center for the Book, 2003, printed by Shari De Graw and Nicole Flores, on occasion of the Truman Capote Award presented to the author on September 25, 2003, broadside 200 signed copies, 40 × 28 cm.

IN 1960 FREDRICK NEWTON ARVIN was dismissed from his teaching position at Smith College on charges related to what the laws at that time deemed homosexual activities involving "soft porn" photographs. Arvin was an eminent scholar of American literature. In 1946 while at Yaddo, Arvin began a two-year love affair with Truman Capote. (Sylvia Plath was one of Arvin's students at Smith College.) Arvin died in 1963. The Truman Capote Award for Literary Criticism, as stated in Capote's will, is given in honor of Newton Arvin. Seamus Heaney received the Truman Capote Prize in 2003 for *Finders Keepers: Selected Prose 1971–2001.* To mark the occasion of the award presentation to Heaney, the University of Iowa Center for the Book published *Testimonies*, part one of which is collected in *District and Circle* as "Anahorish 1944." The University of Iowa manages the award on behalf of the Truman Capote Literary Trust. Another distinguished broadside appeared in 2004, *Höfn*, to celebrate Heaney's visit to Smith College.

In the spring of 2004, to commemorate the opening of the Poetry Center Room at Smith College, the Center initiated a series of fine letterpress broadsides. Heaney's *Höfn* was the third broadside designed and illustrated by Barry Moser, printer-to-the-college. Moser has illustrated over two hundred and fifty books, and his edition of *Alice's Adventures in Wonderland* won the 1983 National

Book Award. Moser's *Höfn* illustration has an almost apocalyptic dimension to it as a result of combining the melting glaciers with a lightning bolt from above. When talking about "Höfn" and similar poems, Heaney said that they are like environmental elegies and not protest poems. Höfn is an Icelandic fishing village near Vantajökull, the largest icecap in Europe and the site of two famous volcanic eruptions, in 2004 and 2011.

Part 1 of *Testimonies* has the feel of a protest poem, an anti-war poem. The title in red, by the Iowa City calligrapher Glen Epstein, references the poem's opening line: "We were killing pigs when the Americans arrived." Images of red continue in the poem in "gutter blood" and "slaughter house," foreshadowing the D-Day campaign. Epstein's shattered calligraphy also reminds one of Picasso's *Guernica* in its allusion to the mangled and mutilated men, the demolition and destruction of the western world. Part 2 of *Testimonies* was not collected, perhaps because it sounded too much like passages from Heaney's early autobiographical prose and poems from *Wintering Out*. Published after the U.S. invasion of Iraq, *Testimonies* reminds us of one role of the poet that Heaney did not shy away from—the poet as witness. Published as discreet publications, the broadsides seem innocuous enough. However, when brought together *Hofn* and *Testimonies* explore two possible doomsday scenarios—global warming and world war. The fine design and handsome printing enhance the poems' darker dimensions.

Höfn, printed by Michael Russem at The Kat Ran Press, designed and illustrated by Barry Moser, in celebration of Heaney's visit to Smith College, October 26, 2004, broadside 100 signed copies, 41.5 × 27.5 cm.

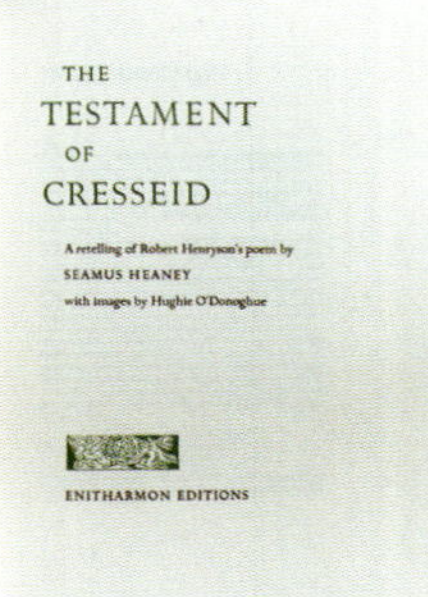

36 : *The Testament of Cresseid, Stone from Delphi*

SEAMUS HEANEY PRACTICED A POLITICS of inclusivity and mutual respect through his many translations and historical allusions. The engagement with other languages, cultures, and epochs was essential to the energy and scope of his own poems and served as important refueling stations on his imaginative journey. Heaney believed that one function of the poet was to refresh language, to reenergize the common idiom through poetic insight and inspiration. Translations were another way of bringing unknown words and worlds into being and of reminding us that "Great Poetry" is always contemporary and relevant.

Four late publications attest to Heaney's ongoing belief in the importance of translation and cultural retrieval and revitalization: *The Testament of Cresseid* (2004), *Stone from Delphi* (2012), *The Owl* (April 2013), and *The Last Walk* (October 2013). The limited edition translation by Heaney of the fifteenth century Scottish poet Robert Henryson's *The Testament of Cresseid* opens the 2009 trade edition *The Testament of Cresseid & Seven Fables*. *Stone from Delphi*, edited by Helen Vendler, is an anthology of original poems and translations by Heaney dealing with classical literature. *The Owl* is taken from Heaney's translations from the Italian of poems by the twentieth century Italian poet Giovanni Pascoli, one of which, "A Kite for Aibhín," closes Heaney's final trade edition, *Human Chain*. *The Last Walk* is a collection of sixteen "madrigals" also translated from the Italian of Pascoli and is the last edition approved by Heaney for publication.

When he died, Seamus Heaney was, of all things, working on an animated version of five of the seven fables by Robert Henryson that appear in the trade publication *The Testament of Cresseid and Seven Fables*. The animation project was completed and has been broadcast on BBC 2, Northern Ireland. (The Fables even have their own iPad app: fivefablesapp.com.) It was the fables themselves that first caught Heaney's attention while attending an exhibition at the British Library called "Chapter and Verse." He was immediately drawn to the image of a cock that accompanied the opening lines of Henryson's fable "The Cock and the Jasper." Following the logic he used when translating *Sweeney Astray* — you can't have the pleasure of translating the lyrics unless you put in the work translating the prose — Heaney decided to tackle the long work, full of gravitas and tragedy, before having fun with the fables.

There is an obvious post-modern distance between the drawings for animation and the etchings by Hughie O'Donoghue for the Enitharmon Press limited edition of *The Testament of Cresseid*. Heaney dedicated the first poem in *District and Circle*, "The Turnip Snedder," to Hughie O'Donoghue, whose artistic image of a boy standing by a snedder serves as the front cover of the FSG edition. O'Donoghue's images share the darkness of the snedder poem, which expresses the tragic vision of *The Testament of Cresseid* as it picks up in Troy where Chaucer's *Troilus and Criseyde* leaves off.

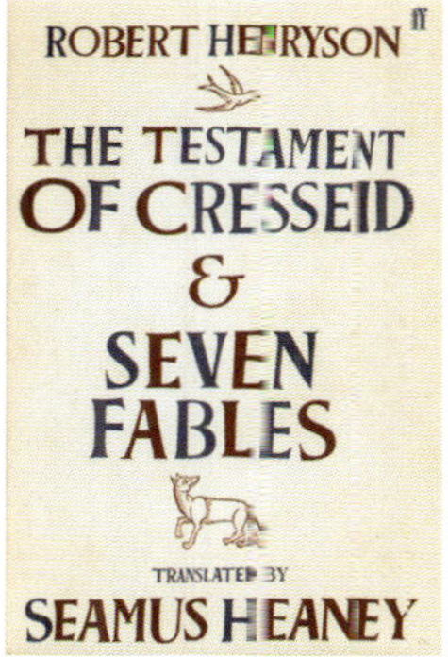

The Testament of Cresseid & Seven Fables. Faber, June 4, 2009.

District and Circle, FSG, 2006, with image by Hughie O'Donoghue of boy standing by turnip snedder.

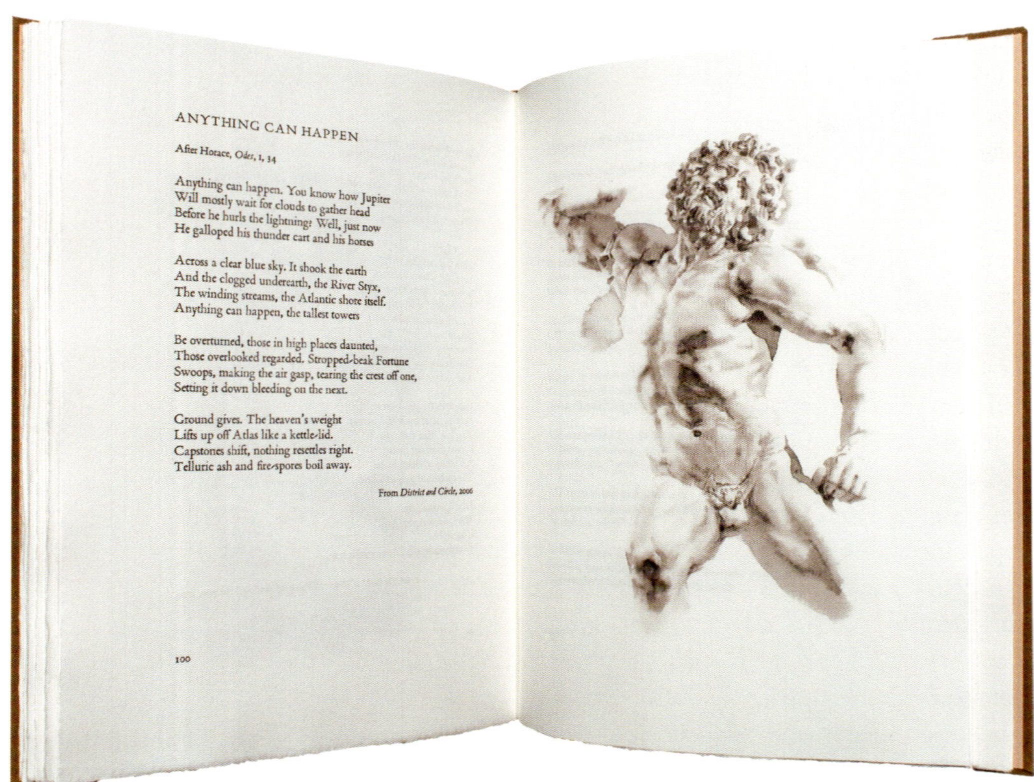

Stone From Delphi, The Arion Press, 2012, watercolor drawings by Wendy Artin, 300 numbered copies and 26 lettered copies, signed by the author and artist, brown and tan boards, brown and tan slipcase, 22 × 30 cm.

Heaney began working on Henryson's poem soon after completing *Beowulf* in 1999. His translation of *Beowulf* draws heavily upon the mid-Ulster vernacular of his home place and "Scullion-speak," the Hiberno-English used by his relatives living nearby. Translating *The Testament of Cresseid* allowed Heaney to continue exploring the etymological roots of his native mid-Ulster dialect and reconnect with their lowland Scottish analogues. Heaney was a physical poet whose intuitive powers found ways of moving writing projects, especially large projects, ahead by making use of opportunities — often publishing opportunities — others may have missed. Heaney needed a way to bring closure to the long Henryson project before he could return to the original place of pleasure in the fables. Thus, the chance to publish *The Testament of Cresseid* as a limited edition came at an opportune time.

One of Seamus Heaney's most enthusiastic and erudite prose pieces on translating, translators, and the power of ancient poets is his 1992 introduction to Robert Fitzgerald's translation of the *The Odyssey* published by Everyman's Library in 1992. While maintaining a scholarly perspective, Heaney makes Homer's world and words come alive in his time-traveling impressionistic descriptions.

Heaney also sings the praises of Fitzgerald's translation, the echoes of which resonate in "In Memoriam: Robert Fitzgerald," which appeared in the *Irish Press* June 1987 and was collected in *Seeing Things*. The introduction to Fitzgerald's translation of *The Odyssey* is one of the few places where Heaney discusses at length what he finds exemplary in Homer and his work. Another place where we are given exceptional access to Heaney's engagement with classical literature is in Helen Vendler's introduction to *Stone from Delphi* (2012).

Stone from Delphi documents and embodies Heaney's love of and attraction to all things classical. Forty-nine poems and excerpts from seventeen of Heaney's books spanning almost fifty years attest to this amazing affinity. The book's title comes from Heaney's poem "Stone from Delphi" published in *Station Island* (1984). Heaney often uses classical mythology to make sense of the world, as in his poem responding to 9/11, "Anything Can Happen," based on passages from Horace. He also uses classical mythology to help understand the sources of his poetic powers, as in the poem "Antaeus" (1966), or the possible afterlives in the underworld described in his translations from Book VI of *The Aeneid*. He is drawn to the classical codes of behavior, the basic themes of the epic tales, and the hero's quest. The drawings for *Stone from Delphi* are by Wendy Artin, an American born artist living in Rome. The sixteen illustrations are based on Greek and Roman statues, which undergo a metaphysical transformation when rendered in the watercolor drawings. It is as if we are seeing classical mythological subjects as Heaney may have imagined them in the poems, both there and here, stone and shade, ancient and modern.

According to one legend, Aesop died in Delphi when he was unjustly accused of a crime and forced to hurl himself off a cliff. Henryson works with and out of the same storytelling tradition as Aesop using animals and inanimate objects to make a point about the follies of human nature. In his introduction to *The Testament of Cresseid and Seven Fables*, Heaney says of Henryson something that we might find true of the translator himself: "These are the Henryson hallmarks, attributes of a moral understanding reluctant to moralise, yet one that is naturally and unfalteringly instructive." The instructive impulse in Heaney's work, aimed at himself as well as others, was balanced by a *joie de vivre* and an appreciation for the small pleasures of life. Though absolutely a man of the world who could rise to the demands of any social or national occasion, Heaney's growing up in a pre-electric, almost pre-mechanized rural community instilled in him an appreciation for the rites and rituals of country life and the ability to find pleasure in the everyday.

The Owl

The Owl, Graphic
Studio Dublin,
April 10, 2013

Where was the moon? The sky
Was aswim with pearling dawn
And the almond and apple tree
Seemed to crane towards where it shone.
Then from a banked black cloud
Lightnings flickered and flew
As a voice came out of the wood:
To whoo . . .

A scatter of sparkling stars
In the milky misting light.
I could hear the sea's sad choirs.
Could hear the rustling thicket.
In my heart I felt a beat miss
Like a cry of loss, or its echo.
The sob dwindled into the distance:
To whoo . . .

Over all the moonlit heights
Wind trembled, sighed and shivered.
Cicadas finicky notes
Tuned up quick, quicksilvered.
(Chimes at invisible doors somewhere
Closed for good, perhaps, against you? . . .)
Then that banshee wail on the air:
To whoo.

Translated from the Italian of Giovanni Pascoli (1855-1912)
by Seamus Heaney

37 : *The Owl, The Last Walk*

LEAVING THE TRAGEDY and despair of Cresseid behind for the
frolicking fables, Heaney in 2013 was also enjoying the pastoral
landscapes of early twentieth century Italy through the po-
etry of Giovanni Pascoli. Heaney found his own childhood and com-
munity reflected in Pascoli's work. Standing in the valleys and hill-
tops that shaped Dante's and Virgil's visions, Heaney was already at
home with Pascoli's landscapes. Yeats too had carried Urbino's winds

THE LAST WALK

The Last Walk,
The Gallery Press,
October 2013,
half title page,
illustrations by
Martin Gale.

into his poem "To a Wealthy Man …" which Heaney references in his commentary on the poem that became "A Kite for Aibhín" from Pascoli's "L' aquilone." Heaney was working off and on with a team of Italian "advisors" as he translated poems for two of his final limited editions: *The Owl* and *The Last Walk*. *The Owl* was published on April 10, 2013, just a few days before Heaney's seventy-fourth birthday on April 13, 2013, and *The Last Walk* was published in October 2013 after the poet's death. There is something so resolutely prophetic about Heaney's final volume of poems, *Human Chain*, ending with the Pascoli poem about the afterlife; that *The Owl* closes with a reference to a banshee; and that *The Last Walk* bears such a transparent title.

Heaney had approved the proofs for *The Last Walk* shortly before his death, but there had a been a real pleasure in working on the translations with Marco Sonzogni, senior lecturer in Italian, Victoria University of Wellington, New Zealand, and others. Sonzogni and Heaney had been in regular contact as Sonzogni completed the Italian edition of Heaney's *Opened Ground* and Heaney was finishing Pascoli's "L'ultima passeggiata" translated as "The Last Walk." The paintings and drawing that accompany the sixteen poems are by Martin Gale who also did the illustrations for a 2007 Gallery Press limited edition *The Riverbank Field*. *The Owl* was published by Graphic Studio Dublin as part of an ongoing fundraising project — like so many other limited editions of Heaney's poems. The poem is cased in a portfolio that also includes four images by artists who have exhibited or produced their work at the Studio. The images by Pamela Leonard, Liam Ó Broin, Jane O'Malley, and Robert Russell seem to have nothing to do with the poem; however, the prints' titles provide possible connections in some instances.

The Owl is haunted by the ominous call of death ("To whoo…") repeated three times as a refrain in the poem. *The Owl* stands in stark and dark contrast to the uplifting images and down to earth descriptions and warm interiors one finds in *The Last Walk* poems and especially "A Kite for Aibhín." Heaney typically finds a way, usually through diction and allusion, but sometimes through rhythm, to make a translated poem "his." *The Owl* is more Pascoli and more Poe (as in Edgar Allen) than Heaney. The gloomy landscape with its pathetic fallacies ("I could hear the sea's sad song") and refrain ("To whoo…") recall "The Raven." The refrain also calls to mind, ironically, the refrain in Yeats's unremitting self-interrogating poem, "What Then," which Heaney can be heard reading in the National Library of Ireland's W. B. Yeats exhibition. There is a languidness and melancholy in *The Owl* that reminds one of Mallarmé's Symbolist aesthetic — an aesthetic antithetical to that of Heaney's. Finally, there is a good chance that this is the only place in all of Heaney's poetry that he uses the word "banshee," the mythological Irish harbinger of death.

The Testament of Cresseid, Stone from Delphi, The Last Walk, and *The Owl*, all translations, would seem to suggest that Heaney was prepared to leave the world behind. Speaking through others in his translations, he passed through the door that stands open. In the final text message (from his cell phone) to his wife, Marie, one of the things he wrote was "Noli timere," Latin for "don't be afraid." This was a personal note to her and not a directive to the world at large. But, Latin it was — another language from another land and time.

PERSONAL ITEMS:

A POSTSCRIPT

SEAMUS HEANEY WAS NOT ONLY a prolific writer of poetry and prose, but also a copious correspondent. Of course Heaney came of age prior to the advent of the internet and thus relied upon letters and then faxes to sustain his ever-growing world of personal and professional contacts. The pen in the hand and the ink on the page, were tools of the trade and metaphors for the mysteries of poetic creation. Writing was work; writing was wonder. But it was always about writing by hand. When traveling, he was forever on the lookout for provocative (if possible) postcards and was comfortable writing on the go. He would sometimes arrive at a hotel registration desk with a bundle of letters and cards ready for posting, and he seemed to know the location of every public mailbox in the capitals of the world.

Heaney's correspondence came in all shapes and sizes, all lengths and longitudes, as documented by the substantial archives at Emory University, in Atlanta, and at other institutions and libraries. The typed letter, like the handwritten one, served various purposes as well. Heaney's first word processor arrived in his Dublin home in the fall of 1993. Though primarily, at least initially, for taking care of business, the electronic keyboard's power and potential were captured first in his poem "The Swing," collected in *The Spirit Level*: "Fingertips just tipping you would send you / Every bit as far — once you got going — / As a big push in the back." The poet continues with images of flying through the air and imaginative acrobatics that come from the fingertips' literal launching of the poem.

The exhibition "Seamus Heaney: A Life Well Written" contains two pieces of correspondence by Heaney from the Smiths' collection — a letter to the Irish book collector and publisher Alan Clodd and the other a postcard addressed to Grolier Club member George Edwards. The Heaney postcard is in response to the "Iter" to Ireland in 1997 organized and led by Edwards. Traditionally, the members participating on "Iters" volunteer to write a commentary about each of the respective places visited. Seamus Heaney picks up on the Grolier title *Iter Hibernicum* by noting he had just completed comparable visits to Dylan Thomas's home and also Houseman's home.

Heaney's postcard to
George Edwards. The
front features Dylan
Thomas's writing shed
at Laugharne.

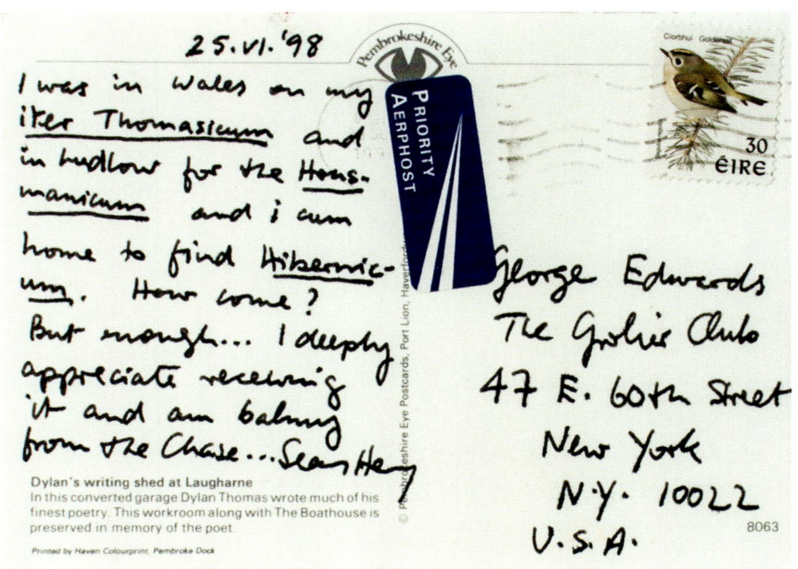

He playfully elevates his "trips" to "Iters" and wonders why he has
received a copy of the Grolier's Iter to Ireland. The sending was a
way to thank the Nobel Laureate and gracious guest for spending an
afternoon with Grolier Club members. The afternoon cocktail party
which Seamus and Marie attended had been written about by Evelyn
Chase. He puns on Lyn's name by referring to being "balmy from
the Chase." Since George knew that the Smiths collected Seamus
Heaney and had also participated in the trip, he graciously gave
them the postcard.

Seamus Heaney's letter to Alan Clodd (March 10, 1997) docu-
ments the awkward situation in which the poet often found him-
self as his reputation increased, especially after being awarded the
Nobel Prize in Literature in 1995. Alan Clodd had apparently con-
tacted Heaney about publishing a limited edition of an introduc-
tion he had written to a book by Scottish poet Norman MacCaig.
MacCaig had just died in 1996, and it seems that the Enitharmon
Press, which Clodd founded in 1967, wanted to recognize the pass-
ing of the Scottish poet. Heaney politely deflected the request by
pointing out that his work on MacCaig had already been published
in Italy. The MacCaig project that the Enitharmon Press contacted
Heaney about was apparently a posthumously published *Selected
Poems*, which was edited by Anthony Thwaite with an introduction
by Carol Ann Duffy.

The core of the letter is a more general statement of distress
regarding limited editions. Heaney tells Clodd, "I am more or less
in flight from limited publications…. So perhaps there should be a

191 Strand Road, Dublin 4, Ireland   Fax: 353 1 260 0807

```
Alan Clodd
22 Hintingdon Road
East Finchley
London N2 9DU
U.K.


10 March, 1997.


Dear Alan Clodd,

You were kind to send me that David Gascoyne book.
Very attractively done.

However, as you guessed, I am more or less in flight
from limited edition publications.  Apart from
anything else, the MacCaig introduction appeared
in such a volume in Italy already.  So perhaps there
should be a limit to the limiteds.  But, mind you,
it gives me no pleasure to say that to a Blackrock
man.  Please excuse me for the  moment.

Yours sincerely,



Seamus Heaney
```


limit to the limiteds. But mind you, it gives me no pleasure to say
that to a Blackrock man. Please excuse me for the moment." Clodd's
efforts were apparently not in vain since it was his Enitharmon Press
that published the limited edition of Heaney's translation of Robert
Henryson's *Testament of Cresseid* in 2004. Clodd died in 2002, and
although he failed in his attempt to interest Heaney in the MacCaig
publication, perhaps he had had the pleasure of working with
Seamus Heaney on the Henryson project.

"Seamus Heaney: A Life Well Written" also includes two letters
written to me (Rand Brandes), an original poem in celebration of my
fiftieth birthday, and a card designed by Seamus Heaney's children

February 1, Feast of St Brigid, 2009, eve of the Feast of St James of Dedalus, born 2 Feb.

Dear Rand

Your chapter, believe it or not, was the first one I read when Bernard O'Donoghue sent me the *Companion* before Christmas, and you ought to have heard from me then. But I'm afraid that after I rushed off a note of thanks to Bernard as editor, the Christmas cards took over - overwhelmingly -and the sense of obligation eventually got lost in the otiose festive season. So it was not only with gratitude but with a pang of self-rebuke that I received your gift of the book.

It was also a gift to me to read the piece again, so thorough in its follow through of the collections from *Death* to *District*. You had a story to tell and told it clearly, gave it a decided shape, made it all seem like 'an advancement of learning'. You made good use of the information about alternative titles – I liked your play, or should I say foreplay, on the first page about the different meaning of 'working title' and on the last page your conceit that the working titles are spirits hovering over the printed pages and influencing them from 'beyond the book'. Not to mention your perception that there is an overall motif of illumination by descent into darkness, from the barn and the forge to the flicker-lit tunnel. I could go on, title by title, but saluting your well conceived salutes to me would smack a little too much of what W. B. called 'the discipline of the mirror', so I hope you will take my gratitude and close reading as, well, read.

Meanwhile, I have a title – as I probably told you – for the next volume (Human Chain) and all I need now are the poems.

With love as ever to Beth and yourself – and the good news that Marie got an all clear when she went for her check-up some ten days ago.

Seamus

P.S— Couldn't get thru' on fax lately – sorry for more delay — S.

in celebration of the poet's seventieth birthday. Even after I had Seamus's home email address, we still communicated mostly by fax or phone. Consequently, when a letter arrived in our Hickory, North Carolina, mailbox from 191 Strand Road, Dublin, Ireland, it was a special occasion. The 2009 letter to me from Seamus is in response to an essay I wrote, "Seamus Heaney's Working Titles: From Advancements of Learning to Midnight Anvil," published in *A Cambridge Companion to Seamus Heaney* and edited by Bernard O'Donoghue. Heaney had often talked with me about the possible titles of his forthcoming collections, and I had kept track of them over the years. As he notes in the letter, I had used the working titles to tell a story about his editing process and poetic journey. Heaney's

22-APR-2011 13:38 FROM 191TU   TO 0018283287204   P.02/02

22 April 2011

Dear Rand

I'm sorry not to have written earlier to thank you for your great generosity at *the Feast of the Holy Tundish, but the* sack cloth and ashes suit the day – Good Friday. I am wearing your shirt as I sit at the keyboard, but not that toothy cardigan – the weather has been glorious here for a week, spring simulating summer, mood-changing, mind-changing conditions. But if the weather hadn't been here to give me a lift, I'd always have your review of *Human Chain –* from its signature master-of-the-titles perception of the prefiguring in *District and Circle* of the title, to the buoyant and perceptive salute to the opening 'courier blast' and the closing 'windfall'. I liked the sympathetic response to the *mythic negotiations* (especially the invocation of Lawrence) and the attention paid to the four-square squarings as a form. You put a lot into the work – Macoige of Lismore *would be proud of you – and I appreciate* the fond tone of the writing.

The shirt and cardigan are a wonderful 'double whammy' – as if I were being conferred not with a cap and gown but something more practical and elegant, the grey stripe and the grey fabric good for the old white head,

This has been a very busy time, with the exception of last week when Marie and I took off on the 12th and stayed until the 15th in lazy and lovely quarters in a hotel down in Co Waterford. Slept a lot when we meant to read, but no complaints.

With gratitude for your birthday gifts and the review, and for being such a sturdy link in that chain, all the stronger for Beth and Blake. Love from Marie too to y'all –

Seamus

TOTAL P.02

letters could be playful even when being serious and are buoyed by humor and humility. Though he apologizes for not writing earlier, it is amazing that he could find time to write at all since his entire country was preparing to celebrate his seventieth birthday in grand style and had made huge demands on his time.

The faxed letter was written a few days after Heaney's seventy-second birthday on April 13, 2011. In the letter he talks about the review I had written of *Human Chain* for the *Irish Literary Supplement* that he liked and found insightful. The other subject of the letter is the birthday present I sent him—a shirt and sweater. Sometime in the mid 1990s while I was staying with the Heaneys, Seamus admired the shirt I was wearing. So I gave it to him. This was the

beginning of a long tradition of shirt ceremonies; Seamus would admire the shirt, and I would gift it to him. Occasionally they were new shirts, but most of the time they were my *favorite* shirts. He is even wearing some of them in high-exposure public relation photos.

SEAMUS HEANEY WAS A MASTER of the occasional poem, the celebratory poem written for the moment, like "A Toast for Rand." The poem chronicles our relationship by beginning with the topic of conversation that launched our friendship—that I was born in the "Casket Capital" of the world, Batesville, Indiana. He then provides the context for that conversation, Emory University, where I did my graduate work, and the Richard Ellmann Memorial Lectures, where I helped cook a pig for the reception with my friend Ron Schuchard. Whenever we were together, "pig" was code for good food and good friends. The toast also mentions the interview that I did with Seamus and published in *Salmagundi* in 1988. What follows from there is primarily about the work I did on the Heaney bibliography and a list of presents we gave Seamus and Marie over the years (in addition to the shirts!). The "toast" continues to bring happiness and hopefully humility.

Seamus Heaney's seventieth birthday year, in 2009, was a marathon of recognitions, awards, ceremonies, exhibitions, concerts, appearances, celebrations, performances, diplomatic engagements, documentaries, interviews, and festivals. Heaney must have participated in almost everything he was asked to do and was constantly in the limelight, a light he did not seek, but was willing to suffer for the good of poetry and the pride of the nation. Generous and gracious—some would say to a fault—he gave of his time and spirit as a sign of his gratitude to those who had entrusted him with their hearts and minds as they journeyed with him through the landscapes of his poetry.

His family celebrated this seventieth year journey by creating a birthday card playfully alluding to the title of his 2006 publication *District and Circle*, which is an underground (subway) line in London. The card is really a timeline of major events in the life of Seamus Heaney and his family. Some of the stops on the line are very familiar to readers of Heaney: Mossbawn, St. Columbs, Queens, Glanmore, and Strand Road. Running parallel to these places are major events: the poet's marriage to Marie Devlin on August 5, 1965; the birth of their children and grandchildren, Michael (1966), Christopher (1968), Catherine (1973), Anna Rose (2006), and Aibhín (2008); the move from Northern Ireland to County Wicklow in 1972; his appointments at Harvard beginning in 1979; the Nobel "dynamite" prize in 1995; opening of the Seamus Heaney Library at Queens in 1996; and his 2006 stroke. Some inside jokes have to do with nicknames, interesting accommodations and trips, pets (Carlow), and

A Toast for Rand

From Castlet-ville he first proceeded.
Now in Hickory he's heeded
As prof. and parent, poetry-guide
Who feeds his poets chicken, fried,
And ribs, well barbecued, and beer
Or moonshine, should you so prefer.
At Emory, in his bloom of youth,
I met him when I fared down south.
In Schuchard's yard he baked a hog
And talked of Toome and Toner's Bog.
He interviewed for Salmagundi.
He annotated words like 'Lundy'!
When Fulbrighting with Beth and Blake
(Who'd crossed the ocean for his sake)
In an attic he was cloistered.
In Moran's of the Weir he oystered.
He listed items A, B, C,
Till driven close to lunacy.
He gave us boxes, birdbaths, rainsticks,
Inlaid gourds and compact discs.
Wherefore to-day I'm dressed in navy –
My T-shirt from the Blue Trout Café –
And Marie's in her Galway shawl
To raise a brimming glass and call
Good health to Rand, twice saved and kenned,
Best bibliographer and friend.
                                    Seamus

"A Toast for Rand" by Seamus Heaney in celebration of Rand Brandes's fiftieth birthday, April 20, 2006.

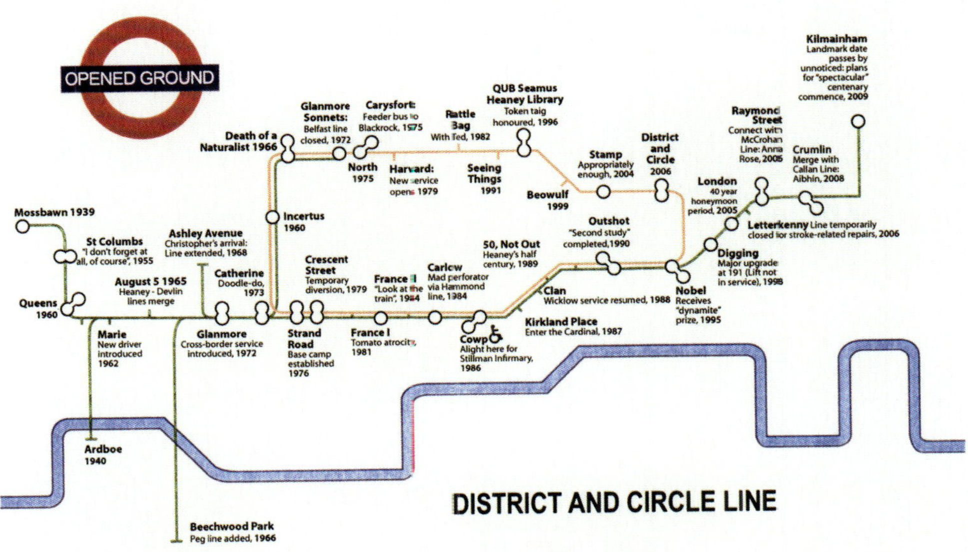

home renovations. The logo in the top left corner of the card combines the London Underground sign with the title of Heaney's 1998 selected poems, *Opened Ground*. The card speaks to the wonderful relationship Seamus Heaney had with his wife and children.

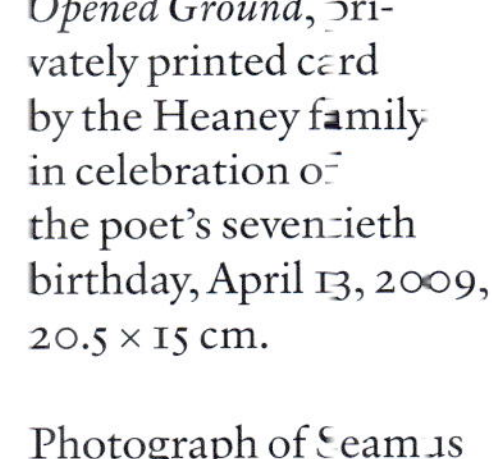

Opened Ground, privately printed card by the Heaney family in celebration of the poet's seventieth birthday, April 13, 2009, 20.5 × 15 cm.

Photograph of Seamus Heaney, Rachel Giese, Ron Schuchard and Rand Brandes, in the mountains of North Carolina, on a side trip during the American Conference for Irish Studies held at Lenoir-Rhyne University, 1992. Giese's photographs appear in *Sweeney's Flight*, and Schuchard is Goodrich C. White Professor Emeritus of English at Emory University and a Grolier Club member.

The Rainstick

for Beth and Rand and Blake

Upend the rainstick and what happens next
Is a music that you never would have known
To listen for. In a cactus stalk

Downpour, sluice-rush, spillage and backwash
Come flowing through. You stand there like a pipe
Being played by water, you shake it again lightly
And diminuendo runs through all its scales
Like a gutter stopping trickling. And now here comes
A sprinkle of drops out of the freshened leaves,

Then subtle little wets off grass and daisies;
The glitter-drizzle, almost breaths of air.
Upend the stick again. What happens next
Is undiminished for having happened once,
Twice, ten, a thousand times before.
Who cares if all the music that transpires

Is the fall of grit or dry seeds through a cactus?
You are like a rich man entering heaven
Through the ear of a raindrop. Listen now again.

Seamus Heaney
Dublin,   Christmas 1993.

Seamus Heaney presented the manuscript copy of "The Rainstick" to
Rand, Beth, and Blake Brandes on Christmas Eve, in Dublin, 1993.
The poem was first published in the *New Republic*, March, 1993,
and collected in *The Spirit Level*, 1996.

In Bellaghy Graveyard

He looked both self-possessed and overcome.
The crowd had gone, the grave had not been filled.
"It's hardly worth my while now going home,"

He told himself as he stood there biding time
Like a man lost to the world in his own field.
He looked both self-possessed and overcome

By something rising to the surface in him,
Old knowledge that his dawning knowledge equalled:
It was hardly worth his while now going home.

Trees were dark orders, earthy seraphim
Tiding and lavish with the notes they held.
He looked both self-possessed and overcome.

As if he stood his ground in running foam,
Having to watch while a boat he'd boarded sailed.
It was hardly worth his while now going home.

As he swayed there in the crow's nest of his dream
Above old headstones and the fresh clay piled
He looked both self-possessed and overcome.
It was hardly worth his while now going home.

Seamus Heaney

1996

"In Bellaghy Graveyard" broadside, 1996. Seamus Heaney died in Dublin on August 30, 2013,
and was buried in Bellaghy Graveyard, Northern Ireland, County Derry, on September 2, 2013
The graveyard is a few miles from his boyhood home and is the final resting place
of his parents and other family members.

꙾

DESIGNED AND
SET IN VERDIGRIS BY
NATHAN W. MOEHLMANN
GOOSEPEN STUDIO & PRESS

꙾ ꙾ ꙾ ꙾ ꙾ ꙾ ꙾ ꙾ ꙾ ꙾ ꙾

PRINTED AND BOUND BY FRIESENS
ALTONA, MANITOBA, CANADA
IN AN EDITION OF
ONE THOUSAND

꙾